PALESTINE AND THE UNITED NATIONS

Palestine and the United Nations

Hazem Zaki Nuseibeh,
Ph.D., M.P.A.

Q

QUARTET BOOKS
LONDON MELBOURNE NEW YORK

First published in Great Britain by Quartet Books Limited 1981
A member of the Namara Group
27/29 Goodge Street, London W1P 1FD

Reprinted 1982

British Library Cataloguing in Publication Data

Nuseibeh, Hazem Zaki
  Palestine and the United Nations.
  1. United Nations 2. Palestine—Politics and government, 1948-
  I. Title
  956.94'054   DS1265

  ISBN 0-7043-2298-7

First published in the United States of America by
Quartet Books Inc.,
A member of the Namara Group
360 Park Avenue South
Suite 1300
New York, NY 10010

Reprinted 1981, 1982

Library of Congress Cataloguing in Publication Data

Nuseibeh, Hazem Zaki.
  Palestine and the United Nations.
  1. Jewish-Arab relations—1949-   —Addresses,
essays, lectures. 2. United Nations—Palestine—
Addresses, essays, lectures. I. Title.
DS119.7.N79   956'.04   81-21143
ISBN 0-7043-2289-7   AACR2

Printed in Great Britain by Mackays of Chatham Ltd

Contents

To the children of Palestine, wherever they may be today, with unflinching faith in their return to the hallowed soil of their forefathers, to rightfully enjoy the happiness and normalcy which I enjoyed during my childhood in Jerusalem

Hazem Zaki Nuseibeh

How then should I describe the situation in the Middle East? For distinguished statesmen and diplomats, my advice is to wait and see the unfolding of events. In the meantime, and because diplomats are a highly vigilant and intelligent community, the best course of action is to ponder, and ponder deeply, the components of decision making in international affairs, with particular concentration on the element of power, as it relates to international issues.

The U.N. Charter is a masterpiece in Utopia. It makes exhilarating reading, and its basic principles and precepts are unassailable. I strongly urge that the Charter be made mandatory reading at high schools, in the earnest hope that we may spare future generations the scourges of war and make them better citizens of our world community as well. But while doing so, we should be very careful not to deceive them by false hopes. We might perhaps write an addendum, warning them not to swallow it whole; that wonderfully as it may read, it is decades ahead of its time and does not represent, for the time being or for the foreseeable future, the real world. And as a consolation prize, it may be fitting to include in their readings a brief compilation of the U.N. resolutions, endorsed by the overwhelming majority of Member States, expressing in unmistakable terms their strict adherence to the Charter and their upholding of its basic articles in almost every just cause presented for consideration and judgement. But a proviso might be added that, in the most crucial issues, the voices, conscience and votes of this overwhelming majority of mankind remain unheeded and ineffectual, because power evidently lies somewhere else.

It is a sad tale which must be unravelled for the benefit of future generations.[17]*

* This book is composed of extracts from the speeches of Dr Nuseibeh. The source of these speeches and the date on which they were given are listed in chronological order in the Appendix on page 196. For easy reference, the list is numbered; the appropriate number follows each extract in the text.

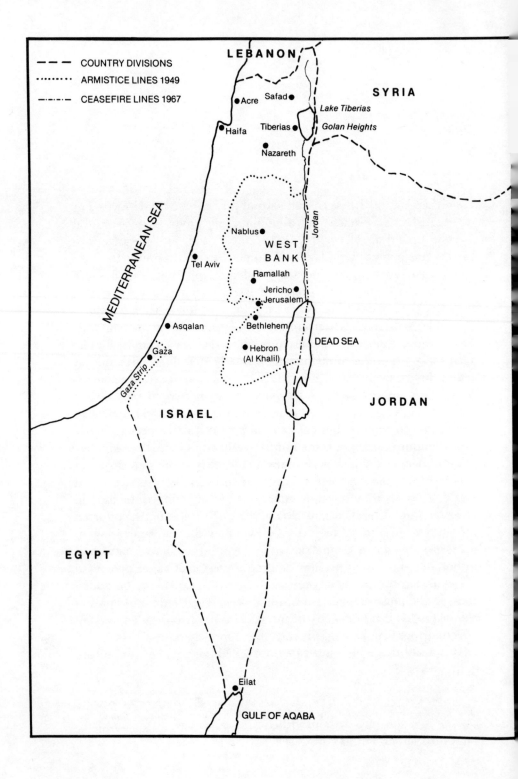

1
The Arab World and the Islamic World

Let me first explain that the term Middle East – as a geographic connotation – is a misnomer. Earlier, it used to be known as the Near East, a wider area than the term Middle East. But for perfectly understandable administrative and logistic convenience, the renowned British General Wavell in World War II changed the name, and it has stuck ever since.[17] It is therefore not amenable to precise geographic, political or even cultural delineation. Broadly speaking, it is the successor to its long-lived antecedent, the 'Near East Question', which had preoccupied the major powers for the greater part of the nineteenth and early twentieth centuries, even though its centrifugal point had shifted from a balkanized south-east Europe to a similarly balkanized Middle East, with the oil-producing countries as the focal point of attention and contention.

Basically, the crisis stems from a power vacuum which in turn resulted from the division of the area into a multiplicity of medium-sized, small and even tiny political entities, carved out of a defeated and degenerate Ottoman Empire in the aftermath of World War I. This could have been totally avoided if the Allied Powers had kept their solemn pledges to the Arab World who had fought on their side in World War I, to establish a unified and strong Arab State in practically all the Arab provinces severed from the Ottomans. The problem was further vastly compounded by a British pledge to favour the establishment of a Jewish national home in Palestine, without either the knowledge or the consent of the indigenous inhabitants.

The Middle East region – strict geography apart – comprises two tiers which are closely interrelated. The first is the Arab World with its close to 150 million inhabitants. They share a sense of belonging to one cultural, linguistic and religious, as well as historical, heritage.[53]

The population of the Arab World should exceed the 200-million mark by the turn of this century – a frightening thought to dedicated demographers; but the territory is close to four million square miles, and is very abundantly endowed in important natural resources. It is not petroleum alone that I am referring to, but to a considerable number of other strategic raw materials, such as iron ore, copper, phosphates, potash, magnesium, asbestos, and others which I need not enumerate. Oman in the Gulf area is reputed to contain one of the most abundant reserves of uranium in the world. As for agriculture, I need only cite the Sudan which has close to 200 million acres of good arable land only very very partially exploited so far, largely because of lack of an adequate infrastructure. It could become the granary not only of the Arab World, but of large parts of Africa and Asia when the nightmare of a world population explosion becomes imminent.

Let us take a look at the actual rather than the potential, the pipeline rather than the pipe dream. The figures are staggering by any standard, even by U.S. standards which dwarf any standards of comparison.

The five-year development programme of Saudi Arabia alone over the next five years provides for expenditures in the magnitude of $142 billion. Most of the contracts are expected to be awarded to American companies, creating, in the words of the *Arab Economic Review*, published by the U.S.–Arab Chamber of Commerce in its March–April 1977 issue, 'vast opportunities for additional American participation. As a result, the return of dollars to the U.S.A. should far outweigh what is spent on Saudi oil.'

This is only one, even though the most massive, of the outlays of the 20 countries which constitute the Arab World. Over the next decade or two the magnitude of U.S.–Arab business should be in the hundreds of billions as petroleum revenues accumulate and the Arab World surges forward in the development of its human as well as its natural resources, thus vastly augmenting its capabilities as an importer of capital goods as well as of consumer goods.

We are indeed just at the threshold of the process with the sky as the limit. But while apologizing for the verbal overstatement, I wish to stress that the substance of what I said is true and not only is it true, it is also mandatory, if the U.S.A. and the Arab World are to cope with the staggering problem of recycling the revenues to be derived from energy and chemical-related imports from the Arab World, over the next 50–100 years. As I stated earlier, it is a vision of the future which should naturally be to the mutual advantage of both sides.

Having given a bird's-eye view of the dimensions of U.S.–Arab economic relationships in the years ahead, I should like to dwell, briefly and objectively, on the political aspects in the political–economics equation. There are stereotypes, prototypes and distorted images as to what the Arab World is, because unfortunately there exists at present an awesome degree of ignorance concerning the Arab World. It is an extensive and contiguous territory which encompasses the countries between Morocco on the Atlantic and the Gulf States in the Indian Ocean.

It may be an interesting historical anecdote that Morocco was the first sovereign State in the eighteenth century to recognize and exchange diplomatic relationships with the new-born U.S.A. As for using the term Gulf States without adjectives, it is because the Arab World, including the Gulf States, call it the Arab Gulf, while our good neighbours and friends the Iranians call it the Persian Gulf because historically, when the Arab World and Persia were united within one great empire (the Abbassid) with its capital in Baghdad, it was called al-Khaleejal-Farisi, meaning Persian. But these are semantic nuances which have no practical implications; as I have always told my Iranian colleagues: we call it the Arab Gulf and you call it the Persian, and both will remain happy.[10]

The Arab World lies astride three continents; it is in varying stages of development; it abuts some of the most strategic locations in the Old World, whether on land or in the seas, and is striving assiduously to reunite that huge but divided world through practical and gradual processes such as a common market, an economic union, social and cultural cooperation and, as yet, a loose commitment to common defence. The process is accelerating, notwithstanding the dramatic and shifting alignments and re-alignments which seem to be so endemic. The common goal is to emerge into the modern world once more after a period of lethargy. The inhabitants of the Arab World are discovering their great past and are at a loss how best to recapture a position of eminence as a relative equal among equals in the modern era, having suffered the humiliation and agony of falling behind in the past.

The Japanese faced a similar dilemma in the mid-nineteenth century and their response to the challenge of comparative technological inferiority was to follow in the footsteps of those powers which had manifestly demonstrated their superior technological proficiency.

The Arab World is probing its way towards responding to the challenge of demonstrable weakness. But, after a few decades in this process, they have discovered, to their dismay, that they have emulated only the superficial manifestations of Western material civilization, without the great volitional and fundamental spirit which enabled the West to achieve what it has achieved.

You may be surprised to learn that the great architects of the Arab heritage at its zenith incline far more to modern Western civilization than to those who want to return to the past whose essence they know so little about. The empirical method, the scientific method, the social and natural sciences and, above all, the deep commitment of those early sages to the pursuit of knowledge and discovery are far better known to Western institutions of learning than those who would want to return to the past without comprehending the real nature of that past. I was reading Ibn Khaldun's fabulous volumes entitled *Introduction*, and I was struck by his closeness in methods and processes to Western thought, rather than to those who would want to resuscitate a few rituals and symbols of the past, as though these were the real force behind the great Arab heritage. The latter are known as the fundamentalists, even though they are far removed from the real fundamental spirit which had given to the Arab and Islamic heritage a place of eminence in the evolution of civilization, including, of course, modern Western civilization. But this is a passing phase, a recoil from challenges which they feel powerless to confront; the cycle of progress in the true sense will continue inexorably forward, as people learn more about their own real heritage as well as the true spirit of modern civilization.

The greater tier, which identifies very closely with the Arab World both culturally and emotionally, is the 800 million of the Islamic World. Some have adjacent or close geographical proximity to the Arab World, especially in the Middle East, such as Turkey, Iran and Afghanistan (presently and aptly called the 'Arc of Crises'. But this huge conglomerate of the Islamic World encompasses important areas in other continents and regions such as Indonesia, Malaysia, the greater part of the African continent, and even significant population centres in the Soviet Union, China and southern Europe.[53] It is an area of consensus, sharing common values, common traditions and beliefs and, equally strongly, common hopes and aspirations. They are a community in the real sense, regardless of geographical location and beyond geographical locations.

They have belonged to this commonalty for the greater part of their existence, beginning 1,400 years ago. The sense of belonging, though occasionally placed in apparent disarray, in consequence of physical separatism, political disintegration and deliberate acts of divisiveness, particularly after World War I, has never been deeply eroded or undermined. For the real volitional force in any area of community is those cultural and spiritual legacies which mean so much in the life of peoples.

Currently, this area is the scene of great turbulence and profound and seething unrest, sometimes characterized by unfortunate and unpalatable excesses.

Simplistic and shallow explanations are proffered as the cause of the malaise and turbulence. The Arab and Islamic Worlds are in rebellion against modernization – as many theorists would explain it, oblivious of the fact that, if there was one overriding factor for the deep malcontent, it is precisely a desperate desire to overcome a relative backwardness which was caused by a prolonged spell of suspended animation and immobility. This has exposed them to unconscionable exploitation, calculated disdain, humiliation and, above all, aggression and threats of further aggression against their domains, their legacies and their most hallowed spiritual anchors. In the age of television, satellites and radio, each and every one of them felt the most piercing wound when he saw and heard Menachem Begin boast and vow, unchallenged, from the lawn of the White House that Jerusalem was to be the eternal capital of Israel, that same hallowed city of God and peace whose forefathers had fought for its preservation and for its sanctity, for the adherents of the three great monotheistic faiths, for centuries on end.

Other outside observers have tried to depict the pervasive and ever-widening turbulence as anti-Western, or even as anti-

Christian or anti-Judaic. Are those same observers not aware that Islam claims to be naught but a continuation and completion of the two earlier great faiths? If they are not aware of this fact then I need only cite one emphatic verse from the text of the Quran, addressed to Muslims, which reads:

> And thou shalt find that the most sincerely friendly to those who believe, are those who adhere to Christianity; for you shall find among them priests and hermits and they are averse to arrogance.

There are yet others who would interpret the current commotion in terms of anti-Westernism, again oblivious of the fact that our area of civilization is not only the cradle of contemporary civilization but is even more specifically the cradle of Western civilization. Religious experiences, Greek thought and philosophy, the fabulous wisdom of the East, the arts and sciences, the discovery of the zero, algebra, optics, chemistry, medicine, astrology, the reconciliation of philosophy and religion, the innovative theories of classical music by al-Farabi, Ibn Khalun's pioneering contribution to the social sciences, and other fields of modern civilization were not only nurtured in our part of the world, but through it were channelled and expanded into the Western civilization of today. Chauvinistic utterances by Kipling and others in the nineteenth century that 'East is East and West is West and ne'er the twain shall meet' was the transient reflection of the arrogant era of colonialism at its peak, when the colonial powers were taking advantage of their undoubted superior skills over an East that was just starting to awaken from its long lethargy.

If my postulates are correct, as I am convinced they are, then why the widespread and rampant hostility towards the West? I would go further in asking, why is it that it was minimal, if it existed at all, in the nineteenth and the early part of the twentieth century?

The reasons are demonstrably political and a reaction against what the Arab and Islamic Worlds rightly regard as persistent hostility in deeds as well as in words against our part of the world and an incredible insensitivity to its vital interests, national pride and very survival. The imposition of the State of Israel at the expense of the entire Palestinian people is undoubtedly the underlying and overriding cause, resulting in total acquiescence in acts of expansion and aggression against the Palestinian and other Arab peoples, beyond the stipulations of minimal justice and U.N. solemn resolutions, and the massive transfer of financial, technological and the most lethal instruments of destruction to an Israel which publicly announces and pursues such policies of expansion unchecked. All this blind and dangerous support, in total violation of the letter and spirit of international law, conventions and the rule of law, has, more than anything else, prompted others to disdain the sanctity of the rule of law, the binding nature of conventions and U.N. resolutions. This is not only abhorrent; it will ultimately lead to a breakdown of an orderly international rule of law and a relapse to the laws of the jungle which the U.N. conventions and other binding instruments had painstakingly been made to supplant.[46]

The truth is that there are hardly any parallels in modern times where justice has been so trampled upon, and where a whole people, the Palestinians, have been literally robbed of every right, including the elementary right to their homes, their homeland, their property, their means of production, even their pride and sense of belonging, and thrown out into the wilderness. They are the dispossessed of the world, the diaspora, which the Israelis have exploited to the point of overkill.

On our side, we have made far-reaching concessions, which would have been unthinkable a mere decade ago, as a price for peace. Anything beyond that would be counter-productive and abject acquiescence amounting to surrender, which neither leadership nor people can ever accept.

Our conditions for peace are less than those already inscribed in numerous U.N. resolutions: (1) withdrawal of Israeli forces from all the territories occupied in 1967 in accordance with Security Council resolutions 242 and 338. Actually, this amounts to no more than one-fifth of Palestine under the British Mandate and gives to the Israelis substantial territories over and above what the U.N. assigned to them under the partition plan resolution of 29 November 1947. (2) restoring the legitimate rights of the Palestinians for repatriation or compensation, in accordance with resolution 194 which the General Assembly has been reiterating every year for 30 years. (3) recognition of Israel within secured and recognized boundaries. To this was added a U.S. condition for

normalization of relationships, which was not a condition for withdrawal under Security Council resolutions, but which the Arab
parties directly concerned have accepted, to facilitate the American
mediation effort and in order to prove in concrete terms their dedication to a lasting peace. And yet Israeli supporters are maintaining a psychological warfare against the U.S. peace effort and call it
a sell-out of Israel.

The Middle East is an extremely dangerous and volatile
trouble-spot. If it had been tolerable in the past to engage in the
deadly game of war (and Israel, I might add, was responsible for
triggering three of the four wars: 1947–8, 1956 and 1967, and the
Arabs for the 1973 war, after despairing of all recourse to other
peaceful avenues, for the liberation of the decade-long occupation
of their occupied territories), the option of war is becoming more
and more suicidal with the ongoing advances in sophisticated
weaponry.

Such a war will not only be indescribably destructive to the
region and its people, but will inevitably have a devastating impact
upon the world economy, not to mention the possibility of its
escalating to global dimensions.

What are the impediments to peace, if war is not the solution?

(1) Israel insists that it shall decide who should speak for the
Palestinians, a very retrogressive and undemocratic request. Our
position is that it is for the Arabs and the Palestinians to decide. We
do not tell Israel who should speak on its behalf, no matter how
objectionable he may be to us.

(2) If any Arab State or group of States arrogate to themselves
the role of spokesman for the Palestinians, then we would expose
ourselves, and rightly so, to repudiation. Since our aim is a just and
lasting peace, then the last thing we want is repudiation, either by
the present generation of Palestinians or the next. Indeed, it is in
Israel's ultimate interest that the Palestinian representatives
should affix their signature and seal on any peace agreement.

(3) The Israelis are systematically expropriating and colonizing
the very tiny area which the world community is earmarking as a
homeland for the Palestinians. Where are the 3.5 million Palestinians to live if colonization persists and is not annulled? This basic
survival question will explode in our faces one day, if it is not
resolved in the interim.[15]

The 150 million people of the Arab World cherish their pride and their heritage, a precious component of the common heritage of mankind, to which they are irrevocably and very profoundly attached. Their attachment transcends their mortal existence. The commitment to a just and real peace must be sought and understood within this context and this context only. I want to make this as clear as I possibly can. It is equally consonant with our pledge to the U.N. to which we all belong.[17]

2

In the Beginning

Scientific and archaeological scrutiny have established beyond any shadow of a doubt that the indigenous and ancestral inhabitants of Jerusalem and Palestine were the Canaanite Semitic Arabs who had migrated to Palestine from the Arabian peninsula more than 5,000 years ago – that is, 2,000 years before the emergence of the prophet Moses and his followers in the land of Canaan. The Jews, or the Habirus – meaning 'nomads' – acquired their cultural orientation, their spiritual experience, their traditions and even their dialects from the Canaanites, the Aramaeans and the Phoenicians, all of whom hailed from the Arabian peninsula and spread into the Fertile Crescent, where they created the five great Semitic civilizations in the Near East: the Acadean, the Babylonian, the Assyrian, the Chaldean and, finally, the Arab–Islamic commonwealth. No wonder Professor Arnold Toynbee referred to the Israelis as a fossil of Syriac civilization. It was from that area of civilization and during their sojourn in Egypt in the reign of Aknaton that the followers of the prophet Moses had learnt the concept of monotheism in place of the exclusive henotheism.

Furthermore, scholars are almost unanimous in their conviction that the Canaanites and their kinsmen, the Phoenicians – they were linked with each other – were the first Arabs to invent the alphabet and to pass it on between 850 B.C. and 750 B.C. to the Greeks, the Romans and beyond. Subsequently, the Aramaean Arabs spread it throughout Syria and the Near East, and it is known by its Arabic origin, Alef Baa' – the alphabet.

It is deplorable that there is a deliberate historical distortion regarding the forefather of all the prophets, Ibrahim Al-Khalil – Abraham. Scholars are agreed that his era dates back to 1900 B.C. It was a purely Arab era in language, nationality and religion, and it antedates the age of the prophet Moses, who came to Palestine from Egypt, subsequent to Abraham by 700 years. Abraham was, of course, a Semitic Aramaean Arab leader whose original roots were in the Arabian peninsula before he migrated and settled in Iraq. This explains why he is venerated as the founder of the Ka'ba, God's oldest house of worship in Mecca. He preached the worship of El-Al-Illah Allah, the universal God whose message encompasses the whole of mankind. The prophet Moses had his origins in Egypt and moved into the land of Canaan during the thirteenth century B.C. His followers deviated from his teachings and followed their own exclusive God, Yahua, considering themselves to be the chosen people.

Throughout the entire period, including the 72-year Israeli hegemony over the West Bank, which is a drop in the ocean compared with 5,000 years of uninterrupted Canaanite habitation, the Canaanites were the overwhelming majority in Jerusalem and Palestine.

The citadel of Uru Salem, which was known as the citadel of Canaan or the citadel of Zion on Mount Zion – Al-Nabi-Daoud – remained impregnable to all conquerors 2,000 years before the era of the prophet Moses and for 300 years after until King David succeeded in occupying it by seizing its water supply, according to archaeologists and historians.

In view of the falsifications and slanders which the ancient Hebrews heaped mercilessly upon, in particular, the indigenous ancient Palestinians, much as the Israelis are now heaping them on the present-day Palestinians through the mass media, it would be an immeasurable contribution to truth and to the history of the evolution of modern civilization if U.N.E.S.C.O. were to form a team of high-level scholars without any preconceived ideas, prejudices or misguided emotions to study the history and archaeology of Palestine analytically and objectively as part of the great Syriac civilization and within an integrated and unified theory of the Near Eastern civilization.

If anyone thinks that such a study would be pointless and would not fall within the purview of the U.N., let me declare my own deep conviction that perversions, misconceptions and outright falsifications have, directly and indirectly, contributed substantially to the downfall of the people of Jerusalem and of the rest of Palestine.[56]

It is little understood that the Palestinian people are an amalgam of all the races, peoples and cultures for whom Palestine, for over 5,000 years of recorded history, has been their habitation and their melting-pot. They comprise the Canaanites, the Philistines, the Phoenicians, the Nabateans, the Syriacs, the Aramaics, the Greeks, the Romans, the Crusaders and, surprising as it sounds, substantial segments of the ancient Hebrew Semitic tribes who as a population were never expelled by the Romans from the Holy Land. They integrated with the mainstream of the inhabitants and became, over countless centuries, an integral part of the indigenous population. The peoples embraced Islam, Christianity and Judaism and lived side by side as one people, regardless of race or religion.

Even during the peak of a short-lived Israeli hegemony, some 3,000 years ago, the Israelis never achieved or even intended to achieve a monolithic or exclusive presence but lived side by side with their neighbours. Many stayed on and are an integral part of the Palestinian people, many of whom became Christian or Muslim. (But this certainly does not apply to the eastern European Jews – the Khazars – who adopted Judaism as a religion but have no roots whatsoever in the land of Palestine and have no relationship to the Semites. Those are the people who engineered the uprooting of the Palestinian people through Zionist ideology. Their persecution in Europe we very deeply deplore and condemn as we deeply deplore that an innocent third party – the Palestinian people – should have been chosen to pay the price.)[45]

The name of Jerusalem in Arabic is Al-Quds (meaning 'Holy') or Bait ul-Maqdiss (The House of Holiness) and is an adjective of veneration. It certainly is not a Jordanian invention; it is the name given to Jerusalem by the Palestinian Arabs 1,400 years ago.

Jerusalem was unquestionably founded by the Jebusite Palestinian Arabs some 5,000 years ago; they named it Uru Salem. Inscriptions found a few years ago at Ebla in northern Syria by Italian archaeologists substantiate this Jebusite Palestinian name and the inscriptions refer to it as Uru-Salema. Thus, it was the Hebrews who adopted the indigenous Palestinian name of the founders and not vice versa. Today, the Israelis name Jerusalem

Uru Shalayem, a forgivable slight aberration in pronunciation.[47]

Therefore Jerusalem was built and inhabited by the Jebusite Semitic Arabs 2,000 years before marauding Israeli nomads infiltrated the city in small groups. For thousands of years it had been the city of the Jebusites and Canaanites, but for a brief interlude of a couple of hundred years some 3,000 years ago. Even during that period of Israeli control, the indigenous Palestinian inhabitants remained the most substantial in number.

When the Caliph Omar entered Jerusalem in the seventh century A.D., it was a family reunion with his fellow Christian Arabs, who not only welcomed him but aided him against the then decadent Byzantine rule. It was the Muslim Arabs who permitted Jews to reside if they wished to in Jerusalem, against the advice of Archbishop Sophronius. The same thing happened when Salahuddin restored Jerusalem from the European feudal invaders masquerading in the name of religious zeal.

The Muslims never expelled or persecuted the Jews but treated them as believers in God's message. It was the Romans, the Babylonians and the Europeans who had expelled them.[31]

Fallacy: Here is a country – meaning Palestine – without a people, and a people – namely the Jewish people – without a country. To the uninformed, the natural reaction would be: give that empty country to those without a country, even though, as you all know, the Jewish people had a hundred countries to which they belonged as honoured and prosperous citizens. I am referring to an age which long predated the Nazi holocaust.

Truth: The country allegedly without a people had, more than 50 years ago, 800,000 indigenous inhabitants from time immemorial. That figure may not impress you very much; but when you remember what the population of the world was 50 years ago, you will agree that the relatively tiny territory of Palestine was not a land without a people; it had its indigenous population in ample numbers; they had their pride and happiness and all the good things that their hallowed soil could produce.[13]

Palestine even had its indigenous population of 800,000 at a time when the continental U.S.A. in the year 1800 had only four million inhabitants. In the eighteenth century, 200 years before any Jews set foot in Palestine, the country, and particularly Galilee, was one of the largest cotton producers in the world, for the purchase of whose produce the three industrializing nations of Europe, Great

Britain, France and Holland, were competing. Jaffa oranges and many other fruits and vegetables were in great abundance long before the Zionist incursion.[51]

Fallacy: The Zionist movement was telling the world that they had achieved the miracle of making deserts bloom; and that the land had been transformed into the promised rose garden. Many in the world listened with euphoric admiration, and their reaction – naturally enough – was: if a race of people could make deserts bloom, then the country should be wrested from those undeserving Palestinians and handed over to the Israeli giants.

Truth: To refute this fallacy, I have decided not to utilize my own perception, my eyes, ears and life's experience. That might be vulnerable to the accusation of prejudice. Upon reflection I thought that the best answer should come from the horse's mouth. I therefore commend a highly objective book by a scholar of distinction, himself an Israeli and, I presume, a Zionist. The book is entitled *Palestine in the Eighteenth Century* and its author is professor Amnon Cohen of the Hebrew University. He describes Palestine from the year 1700 onwards. His sources were basically the Istanbul Archives of the Topkapi Palace, selected documents, local sources in the Shari'a courts records, and Europeans powers having commercial dealings with Palestine, a mere 250 years ago.

Many would be astonished to learn from his book that the so-called desert, without a people and without roses, as the Zionist indoctrination was wont to assert, was not a desert at all; that it had one of the most industrious people in the world; what will further stun you is that one province of Palestine alone, namely Galilee, was so prosperous that it could afford to raise a standing army of 15,000 from among its people, and was even able to contribute generously to the Ottoman Empire of which it was a part.

Without being boastful or ungenerous to one of history's greatest generals and statesmen, even less to one of the mightiest powers of that era, it was the Palestinians of Galilee, under the titular leadership of the Sultan's governor al-Jazzar, who defeated Napoleon when he tried to storm and occupy Acre, the capital of that province.

The truth is that Palestine, though small in size, has the diversity of a continent like the U.S.A. Hilly regions with plentiful precipitation, plains and valleys, with almost equally bountiful rainfall, and a desert called the Negev. The well-endowed areas have always been green and expertly worked by remarkably hard-working and experienced farmers. During World War I the forests were so dense that the Central Powers, lacking adequate supplies of coal and petroleum, made heavy inroads into those dense forests to fuel their trains.

As for the desert of Palestine in the Negev, it is still and will continue to remain largely a desert at the mercy of climatic changes beyond human control. The notable exception is the area of Beer Sheba, where, as a result of a serious violation of international law in 1963, the Israelis diverted one of the important tributaries of the River Jordan, the watershed of Syria, to the Negev area, and managed to water the Beer Sheba area into an irrigated cultivable area.

I would not degrade myself or delude you by alleging that the Israelis did not make significant advances in agriculture, particularly in the field of research. But I strongly and vehemently resent distortions of the truth to serve political designs and ambitions, which have been incessantly made against the Palestinians.

Fallacy: The Palestinians do not exist, and have never existed as a people. Let us take a closer look at history, as described by Toynbee or Dame Kathleen Mary Kenyon, author and famous British archaeologist, or other archaeologists or, indeed, the Old Testament itself, to see what it says. If the Israelis mean that the Palestinians never engaged in empire-building or colonized people, then it is to their credit, not their blame. If they were a part of larger conglomerations, and a very important part indeed, it is because their sights were invariably universalistic and unitary and not self-centred.

There was no such thing as occupied territories. The Begin Government called them 'liberated territories', with the obvious corollary that the legitimate inhabitants were strangers in their own homeland – visitors, temporary residents, perhaps tourists. When the Israelis talk about liberated territories, the question is: liberated from whom? From their indigenous and rightful inhabitants of 10,000 years? Call them what you will: Canaanites, Philistines, Jebusites (the founders of Jerusalem), Nabateans, Syrians, Semitic Jews, Arabs or what have you; but can anybody doubt that they – in combination – have always been, since writing and inscriptions were invented, the rightful inhabitants of the territory of Palestine? I would go even further to assert a historical fact: that never in recorded history, until 1948, did the Palestinian inhabitants ever leave, nor were they forced to leave, their cherished land.[13]

The term 'Middle East' is, at best, a tenuous and convenient geographical description. Broadly speaking, it could be identified as an 'area of consensus', a residuary legatee of a common heritage and civilization. It represents a unity in diversity but with a strong – though oftentimes dormant – sense of belonging and affinity, derived from fourteen centuries of adherence to one community. I am referring to the Arab World and the greater Islamic World, bound together by a formidable spiritual affinity and a geographic proximity represented in the east and north by Turkey, Iran, Pakistan and Afghanistan. It is better known in contemporary terminology as the northern tier.

The well-versed in the history of the area are aware of the significance of the fact that, for the greater part of the last 1,400 years, up to the end of World War I, most of these territories and peoples lived within large conglomerates, including the western wing of the Arab World.

The last such community conglomerate was, of course, the Ottoman Empire which, when decline set in, became known as 'the sick man of Europe'. Politically and geographically it was known as the Near East and it encompassed parts of the Balkans.

With the disintegration of this last of the conglomerates, and the collapse of a unified political structure, the Middle East was turned into a new Balkans, afflicted by dissection, discord and a profound sense of insecurity, humiliation and helplessness, in responding to challenges from a far stronger Western onslaught. This feeling of helplessness was articulated in the latter part of the nineteenth century by the towering figure of Gamal Udeen Al-Afghani, a formidable thinker, leader and activist who preached a resurrection of a strong and modernized form of pan-Islamic revivalism, based upon a resurgent State to act as a standard-bearer and catalyst in restructuring a unified Islamic community. His teachings left a deep impact upon the area and the current movements of Islamic nationalism may well be traced back to his teachings.

During the present century, however, a new movement developed, namely Arab nationalism, whose objective has been a revitalized, modernized and unified Arab World, to fill the vacuum created by the decline and collapse of the Ottoman Empire. It was led by the Sherrif of Mecca, King Hussein, the great-grandfather of King Hussein Ibn Talal of Jordan, in the famed Arab Rebellion. Though it failed to achieve its ultimate objectives, its momentum persisted and its message spread to include President Nasser of Egypt.

Again, the movement failed to achieve its avowed objectives because of external forces, as well as internal parochial forces in the Arab World which had become entrenched. Thus disenchantment with Arab nationalism as the redeeming force set in, leaving the area in search of real salvation, a revitalized identity and security.

Hence, the newly emerging forces of pan-Islamism. All the appurtenances and symbols associated with the movement are an expression of protest against what they regard as unpalatable. They are the tip of far more dynamic and potent forces, whose aim is to create an area of community, a sense of belonging and, not least of all, the capability to stand on an equal footing with other areas of civilization and to ward off a present and continuing threat to their independence and legacy. The outward symbols are basically an act of protest against existing inadequacy, which neither secularism nor superficial modernization have been able to rectify. Thus, people resort to taking refuge in outward symbols to subdue their latent turmoil.[34]

3
The Mandate and Partition

The essence of the Palestine question was summed up in 1968 by Professor Arnold Toynbee who wrote:

> All through those 30 years [1918-48], Britain admitted into Palestine, year by year, a quota of Jewish immigrants that varied according to the strength of the respective pressures of the Arabs and Jews at the time. These immigrants could not have come in, if they had not been shielded by a British *cheveux-de-frise*. If Palestine had remained under Ottoman rule or if it had become an independent Arab State in 1918, Jewish immigrants would never have been admitted into Palestine in large enough numbers to enable them to overwhelm the Palestinian Arabs, in this Arab people's own country.

The reason why the State of Israel exists today and why today 1.5 million Palestinian Arabs are refugees is that, for 30 years, Jewish immigration was imposed on the Palestinian Arabs by British military power until the immigrants were sufficiently numerous and sufficiently well armed to be able to fend for themselves with tanks and planes of their own. The tragedy of Palestine is not just a local one; it is a tragedy for the world, because it is an injustice that is a menace to world peace.[45]   Geographic Syria for thousands of years comprised Palestine, Jordan, Lebanon and present-day Syria. The 'original sin' was the dismemberment of natural Syria under the Sykes–Picot secret agreement, to facilitate the establishment of a Jewish national home in Palestine, without the knowledge or consent of its inhabitants.[19]

The mandate of the League of Nations was inspired by President Woodrow Wilson and others, who objected to war settlements resulting in annexation and insisted that they should be based upon the principle of self-determination of peoples. Thus, Article 22 of the Covenant, adopted 25 April 1922, provisionally recognized the independence of the people of Palestine as a class-A mandate, subject to the rendering of administrative assistance until they were able to stand alone.[47]

The League of Nations Mandate Article 22 actually recognized provisionally the independence of Palestine as far back as 28 June 1919. The Article reads as follows:

> Certain communities formerly belonging to the Turkish Empire have reached a stage of development where their existence as independent nations can be provisionally recognized subject to the rendering of administrative advice and assistance by the Mandatory until such time as they are able to stand alone. The wishes of these communities must be a principal consideration in the selection of the Mandatory.

When the independence of Palestine was recognized under Article 22, the Palestinian people constituted more than 90% of the entire population. The Jewish inhabitants were a tiny, insignificant portion of this population. The same provisional recognition of independence was conceded to Jordan, Syria, Lebanon, Iraq and all the Arab countries which were a part of the Ottoman Empire.[51]

In the early 1920s, the Palestinians constituted 95% of the population of Palestine and they owned, up to the eve of their tragic fall and dispersal in 1948, almost 94% of the lands.[10]

The subsequent superimposition of the secret Balfour Declaration of 1917, while stating that Britain 'looked with favour' on the establishment 'in Palestine' of a national home for the Jewish people, was more emphatic pertaining to Palestinian rights as it went on to say: 'it being clearly understood that nothing should be done which might prejudice the civil and religious rights of existing non-Jewish communities in Palestine'. (Strange indeed, as the non-Jewish communities of Palestinian Arabs, both Muslims and

Christians to which the Declaration refers, constituted then 95% of the entire population!) All the same, the expulsion of the majority of the Palestinians in 1948 and the continuing large-scale confiscations after 1967 of Palestinian lands, properties, water and other resources up to this day is hardly consonant with even the most elementary rights to which every people is inalienably entitled.[47]

Infamous as this Declaration was, did it give licence to present Israeli policies and practices of turning the Palestinian people into refugees and of erasing their rights, their properties, their freedom and their continued existence over their soil?[37]

Notwithstanding Israeli claims for legitimacy on the basis of the secret Balfour Declaration of 1917, Britain herself acknowledged in 1939 what an authority stated:

> The most significant and incontrovertible fact is, however, that by itself the Declaration was legally impotent. For Great Britain had no sovereign rights over Palestine, it had no proprietary interest, it had no authority to dispose of the land. The Declaration was merely a statement of British intentions and no more.[45]

Barring conquest and brute force, the unilateral Balfour Declaration inherently has no validity in international law which categorically stipulates that entitlement of a people to a country derives from prolonged and continuous possession. This applies to at least 8,000 years' continuous habitation of Palestine by the Palestinians.[19]

The Palestine mandate itself was invalid because it incorporated the Balfour Declaration – a deal between two men, Rothschild and Balfour – in violation of the sovereign rights of the people of Palestine, and against their will. It also violated Article 22 of the League of Nations which had recognized the provisional independence of the people of Palestine, achieving its basic objective of ensuring the wellbeing and development of the peoples inhabiting the mandated territories, let alone the solemn pledges to independence in the Hussein–McMahon Agreements.

But quite apart from the inherent invalidity of both the mandate and the Balfour Declaration, and even though Palestine and Transjordan (as it was then called) were included in the same mandate, they were treated as distinct territories.

Article 35 of the Palestine mandate empowered Great Britain 'to withhold, with the League's approval, the implementation of any provision of the mandate in Transjordan'. On the request of the British Government, the Council of the League passed a resolution, effectively approving a separate administration for Transjordan. This separate administration continued until the territory attained independence as the Hashemite Kingdom of Jordan, on 22 March 1946.

It was only in Palestine that the mandate, with its inherent injustices and contradictions, deprived the Palestinians of their independence, provisionally recognized in the Covenant, and created the conflict which has afflicted, and continues to afflict, the Middle East and the entire world.[27]

The Balfour Declaration was incorporated into the mandate for Palestine on 24 July 1922.

In spite of the illlegality of the Balfour Declaration, inasmuch as it was made behind the backs of the Palestinian Arabs without their consent, and even though it favoured the establishment in Palestine of a national home for Jewish people, it stated categorically that it must be clearly understood that nothing should be done which might prejudice the civil and religious rights of the existing ncn-Jewish communities in Palestine or the rights and political status enjoyed by Jews in any other country. Britain specifically requested the League of Nations that the provisions in the mandate pertaining to a Jewish home in Palestine would not apply to Jordan.

In 1946 the mandate over Jordan was terminated, when Jordan achieved its independence.[51]

The King–Crane Commission, consisting of two Americans, had pointed out in its report to the Allied Commission *inter alia*: 'that since the non-Jewish population of Palestine – nearly nine-tenths of the whole – are emphatically against the entire Zionist programme, its implentation would be a violation of the principle of self-determination and of the people's rights though it be kept within the forms of law'.

The Haycraft Commission in 1921, the Shaw Commission in 1929, the Hope–Simpson Commission in 1930, and the Peel Commission came to identical conclusions in analysing the causes of Palestinian resistance.

The British Royal Commission, which had carried out an extensive investigation in 1937, stated:

After studying the course of events in Palestine since the war, we have no doubt as to what were the underlying causes ... They were: the desire of the Arabs for national independence; their hatred and fear of the establishment of the Jewish national home; they were the same underlying causes which brought about the disturbances of 1920, 1921, 1929 and 1933; they were and always have been, inextricably linked together.[45]

After numerous rebellions in which tens of thousands of Palestinians, Muslim and Christian Arabs, lost their lives, particularly between 1936 and 1939 – and, of course, tens of thousands were detained in concentration camps and prisons – the British Government issued the White Paper of May 1939. That White Paper remained applicable until the British, fed up with the problem, handed it over to the trusteeship of the U.N. That White Paper stated, *inter alia*:

(1) The proposal of partition recommended by the Royal Commission, namely the establishment of self-supporting independent Arab and Jewish States within Palestine, has been found to be impracticable.

(2) H. M. Government now declares unequivocally that it is not part of their policy that Palestine should become a Jewish State. They would indeed regard it as contrary to their obligations to the Arabs under the Mandate, as well as to the assurances which have been given to the Arab people in the past [presumably referring to the Hussein–McMahon agreements] that the Arab population of Palestine should not be made the subjects of a Jewish State against their will.

(3) The object of H. M. Government is the establishment within 10 years of an independent Palestine State.

The interim period of 10 years was dictated not by any dilly-dallying but by the fact that World War II had broken out and the British were in need of a transitional period because they were engaged in a life-and-death war. They told the Arab leadership that.

The White Paper goes on to say:

The independent State should be one in which Arabs and Jews share in government in such a way as to ensure that the essential interests of each community are safeguarded. The establishment of the independent State will be preceded by a transitional period throughout which H. M. Government will retain responsibility for the government of the country.

The Zionists in Palestine and indeed abroad rejected the British White Paper and revolted against the British administration of Palestine. From 1941 to 1947 the three Zionist terrorist gangs – the Hagana, the Irgun and the Stern – carried out the most dastardly crimes and massacres against the civilian Arab population, as well as against officials of the British Government.[52]

The British Government, disgusted or tired out by the Israeli terrorist campaign against it and pressured from the outside, sent a letter to the U.N. expressing its wish to give up the mandate and hand it over to the U.N., the residuary legatee of the League of Nations, and requesting the latter to resolve the Palestine question.

The U.N. accepted the offer and, at a special session on 29 November 1947, requested by the Mandatory power, the General Assembly recommended a resolution to partition Palestine into two States: one Arab Palestine and one Jewish with Jerusalem to be established as an international *corpus separatum*. The Security Council was entrusted with implementing that resolution, regardless of any opposition. Thus came to a legal end any promises, duties or obligations arising from the mandate.[37]

U.N. partition plan 181 specifically provided for the establishment of a Palestinian Arab State which included, in addition to the whole of the West Bank, the Gaza Strip, the greater parts of new Jerusalem as well as the whole of the old Western Galilee, including Nazareth, almost all the fertile plains in central Palestine, including Lydda (Lod) and Ramleh with a corridor to the city of Jaffa, a substantial strip of coastal area right up to Askalan port, known presently as Israeli Eskkalan, parts of the Negev and other areas.[32]

The Security Council was requested specifically by the General Assembly to take the necessary measures, as provided for in the plan of partition, for its implementation. Even though this request was specifically made to the Security Council, the Council failed to act on the creation, by the U. N. Commission, of the Palestinian Arab State. This failure was not the consequence of the verbal refusal by the Palestinian Arabs to countenance the dismemberment of Palestine; it was the result of Israel's implementation, three days after the adoption of resolution 181, of the 'Dalet Plan' to overrun by force as much of Palestine as they could, in accordance with a long-prepared plan for this purpose.

The Israelis seized most of Palestine while the British army was still in Palestine and before any Arab soldiers entered when the mandate ended on 14 May 1948 to save the remnants of Palestinian territory earmarked as part of the Palestine Arab State and also to save from massacre or atrocities the remnants of the Palestinian people who had not yet become refugees.[51]

We have always maintained that though we were disenchanted at the dismemberment of Palestine by the General Assembly partition resolution of 29 November 1947, it was the Israelis who torpedoed its implementation. The Palestinians did protest for two or three days, but the Israelis exploited these few incidents to implement their strategic plan, the 'Dalet Plan', which had been prepared well in advance, designed not only to establish control in the areas allotted to the Jewish State, but to extend it to the areas designated for the 'Arab State'.

We witnessed full-scale military attacks from the first week, but its all-out launching, to occupy territories of the Arab Palestinian State, was put into action as soon as British control had weakened enough to ensure success. They seized four-fifths of Palestine even before the mandate ended, and the entry of some regular Arab forces after the end of the mandate was imperative to save the remaining one-fifth and its Palestinian inhabitants.[45]

And let us remember that in those days, and after 30 years of the most stringent disarmament of a whole people – the Palestinians – by the mandated power while arming or allowing the arming to the teeth of the Jewish population, Israel had an organized military establishment of 80,000 Hagana, not to mention the other terrorist splinter-groups, while the Palestinians were totally unarmed and scrambled to the western deserts of Libya and Egypt to buy abandoned and rusted World War II rifles at the exorbitant rate of £120, if they could find them.

The Arabs of Palestine either left their homes in terror, or were forced out at the point of Israeli bayonets, as in the expulsion of more than 250,000 Palestinians from the central towns of Lydda, Ramleh and Jaffa, to cite just a few examples, and not through the instigation of the Arab leadership. I recall distinctly that when the inhabitants of Jerusalem's Western quarters – two-thirds of Western Jerusalem – found themselves utterly and completely defenceless, they decided individually to quit. The Arab National Committee in Jerusalem, which took charge of administration during the disintegration of British authority, did everything in its power, including the use of force, or the threat of force, to dissuade inhabitants from leaving. But what substitute could it offer to protect a whole unarmed civilian population from annihilation?[4]

The world had been brain-washed into believing that the Arab armies entered Palestine to kill the Jewish State in the bud. If there was a premeditated plan of unbridled conquest and aggression against a whole people, it was Israel's ongoing plan to devour the Palestinian people. If there is any doubt that this was the case, it was proved in May 1949 when the two sides agreed to the Lausanne Protocol which would have solved the question of Palestine on the boundaries of partition resolutions 181 and 194, conceding the Palestinian State and the right of return. Israel reneged after signing the Protocol and, having been refused admission to membership of the U.N., the Israeli representative assured the U.N. of his government's willingness to comply. He elaborated his government's policy on partition as follows:

> With regard to the status of Assembly resolutions in international law, it was admitted that any which touched the national sovereignty of the members of the U.N. were mere recommendations and not binding. However, the Palestine resolution was essentially different, for it concerned the future of a territory, subject to an international trust. Only the U.N. as a whole was competent to determine the future of the territory, and its decision, therefore, had a binding force.[45]

4
14–18 May 1948

On many occasions Israeli representatives have used the term 'Jordanian conquerors' or 'Jordanian invaders'. If we are to be told that the Jordanian army was an invader, I must remind you that the Jordanian army was a part of the allied armies; it was affiliated to the British army. The Jordanian army was actually in occupation of most of the key posts in Palestine. However, because the Jordanian troops were disciplined and respected U.N. resolutions, they withdrew a day before the end of the mandate.[5]

The Jordanian army never conquered or annexed Palestine. It withdrew from Palestine when the British Mandate ended on 15 May, and only returned on 18 May to rescue the beleaguered Arab inhabitants of Jerusalem who defended the city heroically until their ammunition completely ran out.[12] The Jordanian army came to the rescue at the urgent pleadings of the citizens, who asked their National Committee to go to Amman. And besides, the Jordanian army came to those parts of Arab Palestine which had not already been invaded by the Israelis, and did not come to those areas earmarked by the U. N. to the Israelis.[16]

The Jordanian army was not an invasion army. They re-entered to save 80,000 Jerusalemites from Israeli massacres which would have dwarfed even the Deir Yassin genocide.[31]

Needless to have to repeat that Jordan did not annex the West Bank and Arab Jerusalem. The Jordan army, four days after the termination of the British mandate, entered a portion of those lands earmarked for a Palestinian Arab State under partition resolution 181 of the U. N. It did so at the urgent pleadings of the beleaguered Palestinians under incessant Israeli attacks and to spare them the catastrophe which had befallen their Palestinian refugee brethren.[47]

When Palestine was partitioned, the Palestinians did no more than express their dismay at the dismemberment of their country by a few public gatherings, a few demonstrations and pronouncements.

The Israelis, having paid lip service to accepting the partition plan, responded by launching their 80,000-strong military machine against a totally unarmed people under the British mandate. Their first organized attack was against the quarter where I lived and they managed, after heavy bombardment, to blow up 25 houses in the Sheikh Jarah quarter. None of the civilian inhabitants had a bullet, let alone a rifle. We were totally unarmed and defenceless. The Israelis pursued their organized military attacks throughout Palestine and managed, by the end of the British mandate on 14 May 1948, to conquer unlawfully four-fifths of Palestine, including two-thirds of Western Palestine and Arab Jerusalem, a far bigger area than was allocated to them under the partition scheme of 29 November 1947.

They also managed by systematic and barbarous terrorism to uprooting the civilian population and render them refugees to this day. This is the sordid background of an Israel seeking respectability and acceptability.[31]

The study entitled *The status of Jerusalem*, prepared for and under the guidance of the Committee on the Exercise of the Inalienable Rights of the Palestinian People, is to be highly commended for its judicious and factual description and presentation pertaining to Jerusalem. It is with this background of appreciation and comprehension that I find myself duty-bound to take exception to certain references to a so-called Jordanian occupation of the remnants of Arab Jerusalem. This must have been inadvertent, because I know the integrity of the members of that Committee. The Jordanian presence in Jerusalem, as I have repeatedly stated, was fundamentally and qualitatively at variance with Israeli occupation.

To begin with, the Jordan army had been in occupation all over Jerusalem and the rest of Palestine. They were guarding the Palestine broadcasting station in which I worked between 1945 and

1948. They were in the whole of Palestine during World War II as part of the Allied war effort. The Jordan army withdrew totally and promptly at the termination of the British mandate, to enable the U.N. to implement its resolutions on Jerusalem and the rest of Palestine.

Prior to that, and while the British still held the mandate and were still responsible for law and order in the city, Jewish forces belonging to the Hagana and the Irgun and Stern terrorist groups had already been rampaging and annexing most Arab quarters in the New City and its environs. The massacre of at least 250 men, women and children and the dumping of their mutilated and bayoneted bodies in the village wells of Deir Yassin, a suburb of West Jerusalem, was but one of the many crimes committed against the citizens of Jerusalem and its environs.

Everybody says that the people of Jerusalem fled their city. Here is the answer to that: who flees his own city voluntarily unless he is totally unprotected and subjected to the kind of massacre to which the people of Deir Yassin were subjected?[55]

The truth of the matter is that some months before the end of the British mandate, the Jewish leadership had decided to plant close to 1,000 of their troops representing the Hagana and the Irgun in the Jewish Quarter of the Old City of Jerusalem as a springboard to be used from within, simultaneously with an onslaught from without, to occupy the Old City when the appropriate time arrived.

And that is precisely what they did. I can never forget those days between 15 and 18 May 1948 when the Israelis went all out from Bab Al Khalil to occupy the city from outside while fighting was going on within. Our civilian population, who had been abandoned without arms and without any preparation whatsoever except for 300 rifles which had been given by the British authorities to 300 policemen who had had no military training, had valiantly to man the walls of the city and fight it out.[5]

The Israeli military machine, one hour after the British High Commissioner departed, unleashed their relentless attacks against the Mascavia Compound and all the other Arab quarters which had not been seized earlier. Having accomplished most of that aggressive mission, they assembled the most formidable units that they had in an attempt to storm the ancient walled city. They shelled it ruthlessly, damaging the Aqsa Mosque, churches and other holy places in addition to inflicting numerous casualties.[31] It was in the course of that street-fighting that not only synagogues but churches and mosques, including the Aqsa Mosque, were damaged. That is a fact of history and there are many people alive today who have seen that and who can testify to it. We have never desecrated any Jewish places in all our history because we would not be good Muslims if we did.

Immediately upon termination of the mandate, the Jewish forces from within and outside mercilessly pounded the walled city for three days and nights between the 15th and the 18th of that fateful month. The Palmach itself, the striking force of the Israeli army, was involved. But they were repulsed by the determined citizenry, largely unarmed and with no regular forces or any regular or dependable supplies to enable them to continue a coherent defence. They literally expended their last bullets and they repulsed the last attacks by using the few sticks of dynamite that were left at their disposal.[55]

The Jerusalem National Committee decided to send a delegation to Amman to ask for help. At dawn on 18 May a contingent of no more than 600 Jordanian troops came to the rescue, engaged in street-to-street fighting and overwhelmed the close to 1,000 Israeli Hagana and Irgun planted in the Jewish Quarter despite the urgent pleadings of the civilian Jewish community. The Israeli soldiers were taken prisoner, treated according to international convention and later repatriated through the Red Cross. They included the daughter of Moshe Sharet, the then Foreign Minister.

It was only natural in ferocious house-to-house fighting that serious damage would result.[31] Churches and mosques were damaged, including the Aqsa Mosque itself, which took years to repair.

World conscience would hardly have tolerated the massacre or expulsion of close to 90,000 Palestinian Arab citizens of Jerusalem, many of whom had by then crowded into the walled city of Jerusalem, in the monasteries and in any space they could find.

The Jordan Army set up a military administration while waiting and striving for a U.N. political settlement. When all those efforts were abandoned and torpedoed by the Israelis and when there remained a truncated eastern Palestine, cut off from the sea, from the west, the north and south, it was the Palestinian inhabitants themselves who requested unification with their brethren in East Jordan, pending a final solution of the Palestine problem.

But I should like to add the following. The Act of Unity of 24

April 1950 speaks for itself. Article 2 of the Act of Unity between the West Bank and the East Bank aimed:

> to assure the safeguarding of all Arab rights in Palestine, and defending those rights by all legitimate means and, with full faith and without prejudicing the final settlement of its just cause, within national aspirations, Arab cooperation and international justice.

This position has never changed, and now that the international community is striving to solve the Palestine problem it is absolutely for the Palestinians to exercise their right of self-determination within conditions of total freedom, in any way they wish. That is a basic entitlement of every people on this planet on which we live.

I must confess that the term 'Jordanian occupation' sounds sour in the light of what I have just stated. A people cannot be in occupation of themselves. The governors of Jerusalem all through that period were indigenous inhabitants: Jamal Tuqan; Aref al-Aref, the famous historian; Daud Abu Ghazaleh, a Supreme Court Justice; Hassan al-Khatib, one of the senior administrators of the British Mandate; Anwar Nuseibeh; Anwar al-Khatib and others, were all sons of Jerusalem and Palestine. The same was the case with the mayors and, indeed, at the central government level in Amman. At least half the Cabinet, half the Parliament and 60–70 % of the army were from the West Bank and the trilateral regency, whenever His Majesty King Hussein was outside the country, always had somebody from the West Bank included.[55]

5
Wars and Resolutions

In the aftermath of 1948, the Israeli Knesset legally institutional-
ized the political reality of Israel by its passage in 1950 of its Law of
Return, granting exclusive citizenship rights to all members of the
Jewish communities throughout the world – one hears of residents
hailing from Canada, the U.S.A., the Soviet Union, Czecho-
slovakia and from all over the world – while closing the door totally
and unconditionally on the right of return of the Palestinian
refugees, the lawful inhabitants of Palestine since the dawn of history.

It is axiomatic that this notorious law is predicated on the prem-
ise that a Jewish State, to the extent that it is Jewish, can neither
offer redemption to the Palestine people in exile nor afford the tiny
numbers which remained any semblance of democratic equality or
civil and human rights, let alone political rights. 90% of pre-1967
Palestinians had their lands confiscated during the period 1948–67.
No wonder that the Palestinians inside Palestine, which became
Israel, remained under military confinement and constraint until
the mid-1960s, and their plight was the subject of yearly discussions at every session of the U.N. General Assembly. They lived
under military rule for 15 years. Those wanting to go from
Nazareth to Haifa had to have a special permit from the military
governor, even though they were supposed to be Israeli citizens.
Joseph Weitz, former Deputy Chairman of the Jewish National
Fund and a leading Zionist, stated his convictions in his diary as
early as 1940 and reiterated them after 1967. He wrote:

Among ourselves it must be clear that there is no place in the country for both peoples together. With the Arabs, we shall not achieve our aim of being an independent people in this country. The only solution is Eretz Israel. And there is no other way but to transfer the Arabs from here to the neighbouring countries. Transfer of all, not one village or tribe should remain.

We know how many villages have been destroyed in implementation of his views: at least 375 villages and scores of towns.[52]

The Palestine Conciliation Commission had been working assiduously with all the parties concerned, with a view to implementing General Assembly resolution 181 on partition and 194 on repatriation. A Protocol was actually signed at Lausanne on 12 May 1949 by France, as Chairman of the Commission, and by the representatives of the U.S.A. and of Turkey. It was likewise signed by the representatives of Egypt, Jordan, Lebanon and Syria, and by Walter Eytan on behalf of Israel.

The Protocol stated:

> The U.N. Conciliation Commission for Palestine, anxious to achieve as quickly as possible the objective of the General Assembly resolution of 11 December 1948, regarding refugees, the respect for their rights and the preservation of their property, as well as territorial and other questions, has proposed to the delegation of Israel and to the delegation of the Arab States that the working document attached hereto be taken as a basis for discussions with the Commission.
>
> The interested delegations have accepted this proposal with the understanding that the exchanges of views which will be carried on by the Commission with the two parties will bear upon the territorial adjustments necessary to the above-indicated objective.[58]

The representatives of the Arab States involved, including the Palestinians, initialled the Lausanne Protocol, which could have permanently solved the conflict almost 30 years ago. But when it was sent to Tel-Aviv for ratification, it was repudiated. A member of the Israeli delegation told his then Palestinian friend that it was hopeless, because every time a return of Palestinian territory and people is mentioned, the old man's eyes – meaning Ben Gurion –

turn red. This put an end to any possibility of a real and meaningful settlement.[31]

Israel is the only country in the world whose admission to membership of the U.N. was conditional upon its acceptance and
implementation of the two U. N. resolutions. The Foreign Minister
of Israel gave a pledge before the Assembly to implement the two
resolutions. The Lausanne Protocol was initialled by all parties
concerned under the aegis of the Palestine Conciliation Commission. But as soon as Israel had obtained admission to the U.N., it
flagrantly and unabashedly reneged on its pledge.

The Fourth Geneva Convention of 12 August 1949, to which all
of us including Israel are signatory, was specifically designed to
protect the *status quo ante*, in territories which fall victim to occupation. It is a binding convention under international law as well as
under innumerable Security Council and General Assembly resolutions. And yet the Convention has been abundantly more honoured
in the breach than in the observance, even in symbolisms which, to
the uninitiated, seem innocuous but which strike bitter and deep
roots into the whole process of peace-making.[9] The allegation that
the Fourth Geneva Convention does not apply to the civilians in
occupied territories is an assertion of licence and lawlessness in
dealing with the victims of occupation.[16]

A historical examination of the Arab–Israeli conflict proves conclusively that the Arabs, including the Palestinians, have persis-
tently sought to achieve a peaceful solution to the conflict, as far
back as 1949, when they signed the Lausanne Protocol which Israel
initialled in order to get admission to the U.N. but which Israel
subsequently reneged and repudiated.

In fact, out of the four wars which have afflicted the Middle East
since Israel was established, three were triggered and premeditated
by Israel. In 1956, it was Israel who invaded Egypt. Why? Again,
the irresistible appetite for expansion.[26]

Egypt, Jordan and Syria, fearful (and rightly so, as subsequent
Israeli policy over the past decade has proved) that the situation
was escalating into what seemed a calculated and carefully
designed plan to conquer and annex targeted portions of their territory, patched up whatever differences existed amongst them, and
concluded a hurried common defence agreement, in which they
solemnly pledged that an attack on any of them would be an attack
on all.[8]

To complete the 'Dalet Plan', on 5 June 1967, Israel launched a premeditated and sneak all-out air and ground attack against three Arab States, members of the U.N.[45] It was Israel's treacherous attack on Egypt which triggered the war, while negotiations were under way over the Straits of Tiran – which no Palestinian had ever visited or heard about – enabling Israel to fulfil its premeditated plans to conquer the West Bank, including Jerusalem, the Golan Heights and the Sinai Peninsula. If anyone has any doubts about Israel's premeditated plot to occupy Jerusalem and the West Bank, I strongly recommend that he read Anthony Pearson's book entitled *Conspiracy of Silence*. In their determination to cover up their thinly-veiled conspiracy, the Israelis went to the incredible extent of air-striking and torpedoing an American liberty ship, killing and wounding 150 on board, to erase all records of their expansionist plans and their secret deals to achieve them. This was not an Arab or a Soviet ship but an American ship, notwithstanding the fact that, without America's open-ended assistance, Israel would not and could not be the heedless expansionist which it is today.

The 1973 war was the only war which the Arabs legitimately started on occupied Arab soil, to evict occupying Israeli forces.[26]

The net result of the 1967 war was the occupation of territories of three sovereign independent States, members of the U.N., Egypt, Jordan and Syria. Thereafter, the Security Council adopted resolution 242, in which it reiterated, among other things, the principle of the inadmissibility of the acquisition of territory by war and demanded the withdrawal of Israeli forces from the territories occupied in consequence of war, the establishment of a just and lasting peace, and an agreement on secure and recognized boundaries. A passing reference was made to the Palestinian people as refugees, a status to which they were to be eternally damned.

The fate of resolution 242 is pathetic indeed. An illustrious and conscientious diplomat, Ambassador Jarring, was involved in shuttle diplomacy for a number of years, until his own patience ran out. His assignment was a dialogue of the deaf and when, in despair, he addressed specific questions both to the Arab States concerned and to Israel, the Arab States dutifully replied to them in specific terms. Egypt and Jordan sent identical answers because they prepared them together. The Israelis, not anxious to be pinned down to specifics, or even to have part of their energies diverted from devouring, undisturbed, occupied Arab lands, reacted angrily and accused Ambassador Jarring of exceeding his authority. I remember once asking Ambassador Jarring in the early 1970s what was the latest in the situation; his eyes glazed and he said: 'I was going to ask you the same question!' He had come to the conclusion that his was an exercise in futility, and he reported accordingly to the Security Council.

When a distinguished American leader of public renown and responsibility was sent to the Middle East to study the situation on the spot and report his findings to his government, he returned suspiciously infected with a revolutionary idea which he courageously proclaimed in public, namely that the U.S. policy towards the Middle East should be 'even-handed'. The statement unfortunately remained as unfulfilled as Security Council resolution 242.

This was followed by the involvement of another distinguished American statesman who was officially and most directly concerned with shaping policy towards the Middle East. The statesman in question is none other than the then Secretary of State, Mr William Rogers, who officially proposed a plan – 'The Rogers Plan' – which provided for withdrawal from all the occupied Arab lands, in exchange for peace. The Arab States directly involved accepted the Plan. Israel, in her own devious ways, rejected it. The initiative came to an abrupt halt, and we are today still debating the question of the Middle East.

In June 1973, the Security Council, at the request of Egypt, convened to discuss the stagnant Middle East situation. I was at the side of my delegation during the session.

The debate took its course, with the then Foreign Minister of Egypt, Dr Zayyat, urging the Council to shoulder its responsibilities, and the former Israeli Ambassador, Mr Tequoa, responding cavalierly and oftentimes aggressively as he was prone to do. The Council having failed to take any positive action, the last words of Dr Zayyat still ring in my ears: 'I will be returning to Egypt, what shall I tell my people? Shall I go back empty-handed?' Three months later, the war to liberate the occupied territories broke out on 6 October 1973 with its ferocious battles, the accompanying oil embargo, and an escalation in superpower confrontation which brought the whole world to the edge of war.

With superpower involvement at such a high level of intensity, the 1973 war came to an inconclusive halt; but with Security Council resolution 338, came a new commitment regarding Israeli withdrawal from all occupied Arab lands, and a U.N. peace conference, under the auspices of the U.S.A. and the Soviet Union to work out an overall Middle East settlement which would be just, fair and lasting. The U.N. peace conference met a couple of times and was then laid to rest. A few disengagement agreements were made to avoid direct confrontations between the combatants, and the situation reverted to its former familiar state of stagflation. I borrow this economic concept to highlight the fact that, whereas outwardly the situation is seemingly stagnant, inwardly, that is in the occupied Arab lands, there is a spiralling inflation of Israeli acquisition and annexation of Arab lands which goes on unabated and unchecked.[8]

6

The Palestinians' Problem and Plight

I received a copy of a letter from an American citizen of Palestinian extraction, addressed to the President of the United States:

Mr President:

We the undersigned find ourselves directly appealing to your good sense of judgement and belief in human rights after all our appeals to the office of the Secretary of State for almost a year have been met with practically no action. In summary, our case is as follows:

We have a dwelling in Beit Safafa, Jerusalem, Israel, which is surrounded by a small piece of land no bigger than four to five acres. Our mother, in her seventies, and a brother with his five young children and wife reside in it. It belongs to all of us. Now the Israeli authorities are in the process of confiscating a part of it and, later on, all of it, to make a playground for Jewish kids, even though other vacant land stands empty nearby. . . Our plea for help in the plight of our family and the threat to their existence seems to fall on deaf ears. It is quite evident that all this gospel-like talk about human rights is actually hollow and empty. Yet, when a Russian Jew squeaks, all members of Congress, all the mass media, all the television networks and their affiliates join hands and practically trip over one another to take up the cause. Amazing indeed! However, when U.S. citizens like us, who happen to be of Palestinian origin, call attention to

Israeli injustice and persecution as well as threats to our mother and brother in Israel, we are told the U.S. Government cannot interfere in the internal affairs of Israel. What about confiscated land? What about our kin? Are they of no account to your sense of justice because they are Arab?. . .

The reason Israel continues to flout the laws of humanity, confiscate the land and oppress the Arab is mainly because the U.S.A. offers it billions of dollars in aid each year. Instead of gratitude, Israel, for reasons of its own, shows arrogance almost always. It is quite clear the Jewish lobby has so much influence in Washington that to speak up against Israeli policies becomes tantamount to the fear of God. In fact, Israel is feared more than God, so it would seem.

Mr President, we appeal with all our hearts to that which is within your heart – love and compassion to fellow human beings – to help our mother and brother in Beit Safafa, Jerusalem, in the hope that your action might in the future build the hopes of the oppressed for a better tomorrow.[30]

Next, I should like to quote from a discourse entitled *A Stranger to the World* by a well-known Palestinian poet in exile:

Thus it is that the world understands me; thus it wants me to be. Our struggle has come to an end so long as I have left Palestine and there is no longer a guardian for the fire. The equation of the world's peace is perfected, and international security has become conditional on my being absent from Palestine and from humanity.

I have bidden farewell to no one, to nothing. A rifle-butt sent me rolling down from Carmel to the harbour, while I clung to God's waist screaming until I lost voice and consciousness. Yet the world has promised me some charity in return for signing a truce with myself, for a truce with a murderer comes about only after a truce with one's self. The world has bestowed charity upon me; it has given me flour and clothes and many tents for me and my unborn children, in return for my giving it my homeland and security. And when I used to feel cold in exile, the newspapers of world opinion would protect me from cold and shivering. And when I used to feel hungry, a paragraph of three lines, in the speech of the president of a civilized State, would satisfy my appetite. And when I used to feel homesickness, foreign songs pouring forth from the neighbour's radio would make departure into a beautiful experience.

And thus the world goes to its bedroom and forgets me. Don't wake the victim lest he screams.

Who has woken him; who is responsible?

Answer: A wind suddenly blows and resuscitates the dead.

From where does it blow?

Answer: From all directions – from the homeland.

And who taught them this obsolete term?

Poets singing to a fiddle.

Kill them!

We have killed them so they have invented another term: freedom.

Who taught them this seditious term?

Answer: Fanatic rebels.

Kill them.

We have killed them, so they learnt another word: justice.

Who taught them this term?

Answer: Injustice – shall we kill injustice?

If you do away with injustice, you do away with yourselves.

We'll kill memory. Thus sleeps the world, thus it wakes. It is armed to the teeth and I am shackled to the teeth. The strong is civilized; the weak a savage. They came armed to the teeth with weapons and the Torah. They uprooted me from my mountains and valleys and sent me rolling down from civilization to the bottomless pit.

Was Israel established by any method other than murder and terrorism!? Thus always it is with the world: rapturous about mass murder, censorious about individual murder. States are entitled to kill their own and other peoples, but an individual or a people has no right to fight for its freedom. If our behaviour is subject to the demands of 'world public opinion' as expressed by manipulated information systems, then the time has come for us to declare that we are tired of our servitude and our state of loss and that we are searching for means of survival!

When we abstain from suicide, they say we are cowards, and when we commit suicide, they say we are savages. When we preach peace they say we are hypocritical liars and when we preach struggle, they say we are barbarians. And are we murderers? Who killed whom? Have they asked this question?[48]

The Middle East is at present suffering the pains of transformation, the breathtaking dynamics of political, social and economic change. It is not the sickness of decline and fall but rather the pains concomitant with a new birth. The adjustment of moral imperatives with the tools and techniques of the modern industrial age always involves a cultural lag and it is this lag which causes the dramatic events and turmoil that makes headlines.

The Middle East, I need hardly remind anyone, happens to be one of the most strategic geographical locations in the world. It is the crossroads of continents; at present its strategic importance has been immeasurably enhanced by its possession of more than half the world's oil reserves. Its stability and orderly transformation have become of pivotal importance to the whole world.[34]

The marathon debate, or should we call it filibuster, over the Palestine question will soon enter its 30th year. Its hallmark has been immobility, inaction, and outright helplessness. One leading American statesman, in response to my urging him, more than a decade ago, to initiate efforts towards achieving a just and equitable solution to the Palestine problem, responded in despairing resignation: 'My friend, nobody ever touches the Palestine problem without getting his fingers burnt!'

The question then arises: what is this invisible power which has within its means the power to incarcerate, intimidate and silence even the brave, the forthright and the free? With a conglomeration of peoples, States, powers and high motivations, which our United Nations represents, and unmatched by anything parallel in recorded history, it is legitimate to ask: what renders our collective wills and resolutions so impotent, so ineffectual, an exercise in futility? To me the only power which is above and beyond our mundane existence is that of the Creator of our universe and He is inherently just, fair, almighty and loving.

Neither the Creator nor His mortal creatures would condone or acquiesce in the gruesome fate which has befallen three million Palestinians, victims of dispersal, homelessness, persecution, mili-

tary occupation, economic despoliation, sequestration and dispossession. Their fate and that of their offspring should be an
unbearable burden upon the conscience of the world.

The remnant of what has been indisputably for thousands of
years their inalienable and natural habitat is now being systematically devoured by an insatiable military occupation without the
slightest regard for Geneva Conventions, U.N. resolutions or basic
rights for its victims.[6]

There is an unbridgeable dichotomy between what is happening
in or, rather, to the occupied territories and its people and the quest
for peace which we [the U.N.] are striving to bring about. To come
directly to the point, here is what is happening: one party to the
conflict, namely Israel, has managed between 1948 and 1967 to
seize the whole cake; the Arab side, and in particular the Palestinians, are saying: Restore to us a slice of that cake, otherwise we
would starve! The Israelis, while playing for time, are systematically and wilfully devouring that very slice which the world community has earmarked as a homeland for the Palestinians. The
process of devouring has already assumed such massive proportions, particularly in the West Bank, Gaza and Jerusalem in which
I am particularly well versed, that soon there will be little left but
crumbs.

Every week the Jordan Government, which monitors developments thoroughly in the West Bank, sends to the Mission [in New
York] a thick stack of documents, reports, statements, decisions and
actions pertaining to what is happening in the occupied territories. I
must confess it is not easy to read those documents because they are
too gruesome, depicting as they do a process of slow death, a territorial, cultural and national genocide, perpetrated without let or
hindrance upon the occupied territories and its people.

In its issue of 4 February 1977, the Israeli newspaper *al-Anbaa'*
quoted a spokesman for the Israeli prisons department who said
that, as of January of this year, the number of prisoners totalled
5,852, including 3,000 imprisoned for reasons of security, watched
over by 1,606 prison guards – a ratio of one to every three prisoners.

The spokesman added that the number of prisoners and
detainees is increasing in numbers and that the space allotted to
each prisoner is 1.2 square metres while in the Hebron prison it is a
mere nine-tenths of a metre. The spokesman explained that,
worldwide, the average space allotted to a prisoner is 8–9 metres.

No wonder the prisoners in the occupied territories so frequently go on hunger strikes.[9]

On 18 September 1977, the London *Sunday Times* wrote, concerning the role of the International Committee of the Red Cross in inspecting detainees and acting as a safeguard against the physical abuse of detainees. The secret Red Cross reports state that I.C.R.C. delegates have filed some 550 reports of their visits to prisoners from the occupied territories. The Insight team states that it had obtained 336 of these reports and inspected 80 in addition. The Report adds that at least 200 formal complaints of ill-treatment or torture were passed to the Israeli authorities by Red Cross delegates. This information confirms the conclusions reached by the U.N. Special Committee at that time, that detainees were indeed being subjected to torture. Furthermore, the same Report states that since 1969 the International Red Cross has agreed to modify their reports on complaints and to substitute these with generalizations. The reason attributed by the *Sunday Times* for these modifications was because some of the I.C.R.C. reports, 'had been leaked at the United Nations'. Simultaneously, the International Red Cross had apparently agreed that before any of its delegates would take up any complaint of torture, the person concerned must first be willing to repeat his allegations to Israeli army officers, who would cross-question the person. Since this agreement between I.C.R.C. and the Israeli authorities was made, complaints of torture dropped to an average of about six a year. Now those hapless detainees know and are warned that if they open their mouths and divulge their torture they will be subjected to even more heinous tortures – how would you expect them but to keep their agony within themselves?[16]

The General Assembly, as a concrete expression of its profound concern for those suffering torture, brutalities, solitary confinement and degradation in cells 60 centimetres long by 80 centimetres wide and 60 centimetres in height, might wish to recommend that copies of the Universal Declaration of Human Rights be distributed to both the sadistic tormentors as an eye-opener, and to the tormented as spiritual consolation and a message that the world knows and shares their suffering.

There are 30 such fiendish prisons at the disposal of the Israeli occupation authorities, in which thousands of Palestinian Arab prisoners have suffered and continue to suffer indescribable torture at the hands of their tormentors. These are in addition to collective concentration camps which the occupation authorities had improvised in the heart of the scorching desert to confine thousands of Palestinians, when the prisons, incredibly overcrowded, could absorb no more.

(1) The Mascobiya Prison, in the heart of Jerusalem, is one of the more notorious with 500 inmates and special torture chambers which use sophisticated, as well as rudimentary, methods. These include heavy sticks, iron bars, leather whips, alongside electric shock devices, trained savage dogs and chemical contraptions. No wonder it has gained the infamous name of 'the slaughter house' by those who have been to it.

(2) The other equally notorious prison for Arab prisoners and those arrested by administrative decree is Sarafand which houses 2,000 Arab men and women and is under the direct jurisdiction of Israeli military intelligence. Here is where interrogations are carried out. One of its additional methods of torture is to hang the prisoner from poles erected for this purpose for a long duration then, after savage beating, he is forced to crawl naked on protruding and sharpened stone. As a result of exhaustion and fatigue, the prisoner finds himself moving across and falling onto these sharpened stones which needle his naked body.

(3) The infamous Ramleh prison, located between Lydda and Ramleh. This is called by the prisoners the 'vatrine' because of the frequent visitors to it. But it hides behind it the inner confinement cells which no one could see. The two-floor prison can accommodate 3,000 Arab political prisoners and Israelis convicted of crimes.

(4) The most terrifying prison is Asqualan, it is earmarked for those sentenced to life. It has numerous confinement cells and very high humidity, which has led to serious deterioration of the health of the prisoners.

(5) Nevi Tertsa, newly built two kilometres from the existing Ramleh prison, is allocated to women prisoners, where Arab women detained for political reasons find themselves side by side with Israeli prostitutes and others convicted on criminal charges.

(6) In Nablus at the old British Teggart building where at least 500 prisoners are constantly detained, it is notorious for its solitary confinement rooms 'four' and 'five' where the most brutal tortures are carried out. Often the screams of the tortured are heard in surrounding areas.

(7) The prison in Hebron, divided into two parts, one for women, the other for men, exceeds Asqalan prison in congestion since a mere one square metre is allocated to every prisoner or to the administratively detained. The prisoners, men and women, are rarely less than 1,000.

(8) The Beer Sheba prison comprises on the average around 700 prisoners and sometimes reaches the 1,000 mark.

(9) Talmoun prison near Beit Leed is allocated to children below age. It houses 500 Arab children and 300 Israeli children.

(10) The Gaza Central Prison accommodates 1,000 prisoners and has 26 solitary-confinement cells. Torture is carried out during the night and the victims are prevented from sleeping during day-time.

(11) Shata prison in Beissaan in the Jordan Valley where heat climbs during the summer to 40° C. Again, psychological and physical torture are practised to break the prisoners' wills before the start of interrogation.

(12) The prison of Daamoun in the hills of Karmel near Kibbutz Beit 'Uun. It can accommodate 300 prisoners.

(13) Nebi Saleh prison.

(14) Ma'Siyaho prison, again near Ramleh town.

(15) Tel-Mond.

(16) Beit Leed (Kfar Yona) 10 kilometres from the Arab town of Tulkarm.

Since it is far from my intention to turn anybody's stomach by describing the unique attributes of the remaining 22 prisons, I will confine myself to mentioning their names, in case any tourist wishes to identify the other face of Israel and the occupied territories. The names of the other prisons are: Yaajuur, Damareen, Khudeira, Atleet, 'Aqra, 'Afoulah, Jericho, Tulkarm, Jenin, Bethlehem, Ramallah, Beit Shams, Bassa, Jalamah, Abu Kabir, Rosh Bina, Safad, Acre, Nazareth, Haifa, Rafah and Khan Unis prisons.

These are in addition to many concentration camps and labour camps located in faraway desert areas including Sinai which had, up to 1971, al-Nakhl, abu-Zinha and Qusayha and new ones which are still operative such as Bayyuuk to the north of Rafah, Um el-Kilaab camp also north of Rafah, and Mashru' 'Aamer camp to the east of Rafah; and yet another in the area of Abu Rdaiss in Sinai. These contain over 5,000 detainees. No wonder Israel is asking several billion dollars from the American taxpayer for relocation of military installations, settlements and concentration camps. They are also asking for three to nine months for withdrawal when the occupation in 1967 took a couple of days.

The patterns of torture and brutality have been so widespread that they have become common knowledge, almost impossible to cover up or deny. In many instances, torture, no matter how heinous, brings to the Israelis no rewards, either because of the extraordinary endurance of the suspect under interrogation, or simply because he has nothing to disclose, and his conscience does not permit him to accuse innocent third parties. An example of this is the case of Rashaad Muhammad al-Sagheer from Hebron who suffered interrogation at Mascobiya compound in Jerusalem. He was brutally beaten and burnt in the stomach until he fell to the ground from exhaustion, but still insisting: 'I have nothing to reveal and I cannot accuse anyone.' Or Fahmi al-Hammouri, a construction contractor who, in spite of the torture, had nothing to disclose.

Strong-willed prisoners who may be involved in resisting the occupation remain steadfast in spite of heavy torture. One example is Sulaiman al-Najaab, who was stripped naked and beaten on his genitals intermittently for four hours. He was also told that his wife would be sexually assaulted and was made to hear her voice. He determined that if he did not remain steadfast, the wives of his comrades would suffer a similar agony. He was expelled across the demarcation line on 28 February 1975.

A researcher who has interviewed hundreds of Palestinian prisoners about Israeli patterns of brutality in Israeli prisons and who has kept his name anonymous for fear of reprisals has written a terrifying account of the brutality in prison jails in a series of articles published in *Al-Ra'i*, one of Jordan's leading newspapers. The brutality, says the author, is only matched in magnitude by the enormity of the endurance which Palestinian prisoners have displayed.

Indeed, they have turned the jails into a new area for struggle against occupation, including hunger strikes which, in one instance, lasted for 70 days.

The Israelis never recognize a Palestinian as a prisoner of war, no matter what the circumstances of his capture. They treat him indiscriminately as a criminal, not even as a human being.

Following are but some of the specific cases of brutality and torture:

(1) Salem ben Jaad 'Ubeid from Bethlehem was admitted to a mental asylum as a result of indiscriminate beatings on sensitive parts of his backbone and head which left him unconscious. They had come to arrest his brother and he himself was asleep and had committed no offence. The Shen Bet secret service prevented his mother and sister from giving him any aid.

(2) Abdul Muttalib Abu Rmeilah was tortured with electric shocks and heavy sticks. They beat him as hard as they could; one of his torturers, Haim, was wearing a red shirt. Ever since, he has suffered hysterical attacks whenever he saw a red colour. He was imprisoned for ten years and, because of injuries to his nervous system, he became blind.

(3) Subhi Na'rani was hanged from the iron bar of the cell window and beaten by six jailers, while Ziyaad 'Ashour was beaten seven strokes every minute by seven jailers. Twenty jailers, including officers, participated in the savage beating of Yusuf-al-Hamdan.

(4) 'Abla Taha was beaten while lying bleeding, on the floor from exhaustion. She was two months pregnant.

(5) Ahmad Hudhud related how he was beaten with a wide but fine leather whip. This leaves marks on the body for one hour, but they then disappear. However, it leaves internal wounds below the skin, leading to internal infections and serious afflictions. It is designed to conceal signs of torture before medical committees.

(6) Najeeb Saleem Mahmoud was beaten on the healing wound on his body where he had undergone a surgical operation in his gall-bladder. This could have led to disruption of the operation with fatal consequences.

(7) Abdullah bani Na'eem was subjected to a double beating as he was forced to stand with his face to the wall. Every stroke on his back inevitably meant another to his face banging against the wall. The interrogation and brutality inflicted on this man lasted for six months.

(8) Abdul-Jaaber Assuyuri was ordered to take off his clothes, then his hands were chained behind his back and he was hung up by a rope attached to his body and the ceiling. Dangling naked, he was beaten savagely on sensitive parts of his body.

(9) Jameel al-Hassan was chained in his solitary-confinement cell, and next to him was placed one of the prison warders whose job it was to beat the prisoner whenever he became sleepy.

(10) Fendi Faaris was tortured by burning paper placed between the toes. His skin would burn and be consumed, along with the burning paper, and all the while the torturers were wheedling with Faaris to confess.

(11) Abdullah Yuusef 'Adwan was crucified in the Tulkarm prison where his jailers would light up matches, one after the other, and place them on his lip, until they began to melt. The same was applied to Abdul Muttalib Abu Rmeila. Engineer Husni Haddad had lighted cigarettes stubbed out against the skin of his feet. The agony was such that he became unable to move or walk.

(12) Israel Shahaak, writing in *al-Ittihad*, which is published in Israel, described the tragedy which had afflicted Shawqi al-Khateeb. Shawqi was confined to a cell, and every 15 minutes a jailer would take him to an adjacent room where electric shocks were applied. After every electric shock he would be stripped naked and sprayed with cold water to intensify the pain. The alternation of electricity and water could be fatal. The application of electric shocks on Ziyaad 'Ashour resulted in paralysis of his left arm. A more ingenious method was to tie the prisoner, Ziyaad el-'Azzeh, to a seat, connect electric leads to the lobes of his ears and switch on the current with simultaneous loud telephone shrieks. The shrieks and the electric currents resulted in permanent and intolerable pain in Ziyaad's head.

Another pattern of torture would be to hang a prisoner to the wall with his hands chained. As he dangles unprotected, his bodily weight has to be born by his hands, and torture begins. In the case of Abdul-Salaam el-Tamimi his wrists were chained to the sharp edges of the door of the cell. Every time he tried to relax his wrists would be pierced and wounded by the sharp edges. It was preferable for him to keep his hands hung and tied to avoid the sharp edges.

Sulayman al-Najaab and Yusuf el-Ali remained for 32 days chained in a confinement cell 60 centimetres by 60 and a height of 160 centimetres. The floor of the cell had sharp edges. They were forced to crawl to the torture chambers with faces covered by jute bags and hands folded behind their backs.

Torture by chemicals is by no means neglected. Atta al-Qamari was given an injection in his sexual organ and told that the injection would transform him into a woman. He lost consciousness and, when he recovered, they beat him on the genitals. Ahmad

Hudhud was also injected in the vein which resulted in a swelling of his head skin. He was operated on in hospital but the operation failed to remove the liquid from his head. He eventually lost his sight.

Even sulphuric acid was applied in certain instances leading to unbearable pain.

It is agonizing to me to read about such practices, but for the fact that these are not horror stories prepared for the screen or hair-raising novels. They relate the real story and involve the flesh, blood and soul of real human beings, many of whom have survived their firmament and are now outside the occupied territories, quite ready to narrate their tale.

The plea of non-accountability and the claims of simply carrying out orders from superiors were rejected by the Nuremberg Tribunal after World War II. It should be made expressly clear that all the individuals involved in acts of atrocities against hapless prisoners of conscience and of right should not be exonerated from personal accountability, in every case where sadistic aberrations, zealotry and blind hate moved them to behave in excess of their duties, whether as jailers or as interrogators. This is what human rights are about and is the acid test in disentangling politics and decent human behaviour.[25]

The Arab World and the Palestinian people have made it amply clear that they are willing to settle the conflict on a just and equitable basis which would enable both peoples to work together and live together in peace and cooperation.

The real challenge is posed by Israel's declared policy of conceding no meaningful rights to the Palestinian people. Is Israel strategically interested in a just and lasting peace with its neighbours, or is its ultimate goal territorial expansion and acquisition, at a moment in history when practically the entire world, including tiny islands, has been decolonized?[53]

Time is Israel's most precious commodity to fulfil its longstanding designs to take over the whole of Palestine and well beyond, as circumstances permit. The whole game is a race against time, to confront the world with a new *fait accompli*. Israel has set its navigational instruments in pursuance of its goals of 'expanded conflict' and not peaceful co-existence based on mutual benefit. That this is, in the final analysis, a collision course, a time-bomb which can lead only to an 'expanded explosion', is cavalierly and ominously relished and spelt out, in the book entitled *None Will Survive Us: The Story of the Israeli A-Bomb*, by Eli Teicher and Ami Dor-On, two Israeli journalists, whose book the Israeli military censor, General Shani, has banned and barred to publication. The A-bomb development has been the accomplishment of an Israeli–South African collaboration since the mid-1960s, because both are united in their common goal of blackmailing and subjugating the vast masses of humanity in Asia and Africa.[51]

It is now conclusively evident after 30 years that raw power, not an orderly international system, sways the day, unrestrained by considerations of justice, equity and U.N. resolutions. Any redemption for the Palestinian people must therefore be sought through other avenues, if not in this generation, then in generations to come. For the 3.5 million Palestinian Arabs, it is a long, long struggle for survival. And they will not fade away from off the face of the earth, no matter what happens now or then.

Feverish and breathtaking diplomatic activity is presently under way on almost all fronts, but with varying approaches, forms and attitudes. Having been the victims and the pawns in the game for decades, however, the Palestinian people have lost faith in forms, approaches and attitudes. They can only have their faith restored when they see, in concrete and tangible form, that their existence is no longer in imminent jeopardy; that, like all other nations of the world, they have a homeland and a place which they can call their own; that they can live in dignity, normalcy and freedom, not on borrowed time and not in the wilderness.

Pending that day, it is our duty as members of the U.N. to continue to give unequivocal support to a people afflicted by unparalleled adversity.

It is truly surprising that the Israelis, who claim to want peace and live peacefully with their closest neighbours – the Palestinians – are fearful of an across-the-table dialogue with their principal adversaries, who have indicated their willingness for such a dialogue.

If serious consideration was given by the Israeli leadership to the uppermost questions of peace, and if the Palestinians and Israelis live side by side in amity and fraternity, as the Arabs and the Jews did for countless generations, the Middle East and the world might well witness one of its greatest creative transformations. A decision either way will be momentous for all. But this can only happen if both of us unshackle ourselves from the conflicts, tragedies and sufferings of the past few decades.[18]

7

The Israeli Response
to U.N. Resolutions

The unalterable and natural position of the General Assembly over the decades has been that every Palestinian refugee is *ipso facto* entitled to return to his home and to live at peace with his neighbours. Those not choosing to return should be entitled to full compensation. Indeed, in a resolution of December 1949, the General Assembly had visualized an early termination of direct relief by 31 December 1950.[58]

The Charter of the U.N. and the authority vested in its executive arm, the Security Council, should have seen to it, more than a decade ago, that occupation, aggression and massive violation of all the human rights of the population under occupation, protected under the Fourth Geneva Convention of 1949, would have been terminated forthwith, in accordance with the Security Council resolution itself. Failing this, the provisions of Chapter VII should have been applied against the recalcitrant party. The vetoes at the Security Council by certain major powers have notoriously paralysed the efficacy of an international order as enshrined by the founders of the Charter. Instead, a calculated policy of procrastination, delays and endless debates rendered the Security Council and, hence, the U.N. system a lame duck, and afforded the Zionist entity the precious time it most needed to colonize and subjugate the occupied lands and its people, while the world watched with agonized frustration and helplessness, as the effectiveness of the world body dwindled under the devastating blows of its own impotence.

No wonder even attendance and participation at U.N. deliberations has fallen to an all-time low.

Resolution 194 of 11 December 1948 and 394 of 14 December
1950, both sponsored by the U.S.A. and other Member States,
upheld the right of the Palestine refugees to repatriation to Palestine. They also upheld the right of every Palestinian who may not
opt to return to full compensation. They also provided for the
protection of the rights, property and interests of the Palestine
refugees, pending their return. Resolution 194 has been reiterated
every year for the past 30 years, and the U.N. in its entirety is
legally and morally bound to carry it out. And yet these resolutions
have remained ink on paper. Not a single refugee has exercised his
right to return; and all Palestinian rights, properties and interests
have been confiscated and distributed at nominal or no cost to
newly arriving alien immigrants, who under all laws of equity and
justice have not the remotest entitlement to them. If this is not
highway robbery, what is?[27]

When Israel laid claims to Arab Jerusalem and the rest of the
West Bank on untenable and spurious historical interpretations
which, naturally, shocked the rest of the world, the Israelis reverted
to their time-honoured 'security' argument, alleging that their
so-called security required, and Security Council resolution 242
permitted, continued and permanent Israeli military occupation of
the West Bank, under varying forms, modalities and guises. That
Security Council resolution 242 specifically mandated Israeli withdrawal; that the said resolution explicitly stated the inadmissibility
of the acquisition of territory by force; that the Charter and the
Fourth Geneva Convention of 1949 strictly forbid any tampering
with the inviolability of the territories under occupation and the
violation of basic human rights of their people; all these banal and
universally recognized facts are arrogantly and cavalierly dismissed
as irrelevant and a nuisance. If this is how Israel treats everything
that emanates from the world community, then what moral or legal
entitlement does Israel have to justify its continued membership of
the U.N. – the more so when it is recalled that it is the only country
in the world whose admission in the first place was made conditional upon its compliance with the right to return of the Palestinians under resolution 194 and a territorial settlement on the basis
of resolution 181.[26]

Israel alleged that Security Council resolutions 242 and 338 have annulled previous U.N. resolutions. This is a very strange and twisted reading of the situation. Resolution 242 was intended to deal with the consequences of the 1967 war, and there is nothing there or elsewhere which provided for abrogation of long-established U.N. resolutions.

Indeed, the Security Council has no jurisdiction to abrogate U.N. resolutions, particularly General Assembly resolutions, nor does the Security Council lay any claims to such jurisdiction.[16]

Israel continues to insist that its security is threatened while it occupies territory ten times the amount originally allocated to it in 1947. In spite of this, the Arab States directly involved, have, for the past 10 years, been willing to negotiate a just peace on the basis of Security Council resolution 242, based on terminating all claims or states of belligerency, and guarantees of the territorial inviolability and independence of all States in the area. Israel, as usual, paid lip service to the resolution, while torpedoing it effectively on the ground. The whole game was a race against time, to confront the world with a new *fait accompli*. Time is Israel's most precious commodity, or so it calculates, to enable it to bring in new immigrants, sequestrate as much land as it can absorb and thus fulfil its longstanding ambition to take over the whole of Palestine, and far beyond, as circumstances may permit.[26]

What do Articles 1 and 2 of the Charter have to say about illegal acquisitions and occupations? During the Israeli, French and British invasion of Egypt in 1956, a great President of the U.S.A., President Eisenhower, in a radio and television address on 20 February 1957 explained them categorically:

> The use of military force to solve international disputes could not be reconciled with the principles and purposes of the U.N. We are approaching a fateful moment when either we must recognize that the U.N. is unable to restore peace in this area, or the U.N. must renew with increased vigour its efforts to bring about Israeli withdrawal.
>
> Israel seeks something more. It insists on firm guarantees as a condition to withdrawing its forces of invasion. This raises a basic question of principle. Should a nation which attacks and occupies foreign territory in the face of U.N. disapproval be allowed to impose conditions on its own withdrawal?
>
> We cannot consider that the armed invasion and occupation

of another country are 'peaceful means' or 'proper means' to
achieve justice and conformity with international law. But the
U.N. faces immediately the problem of what to do next. If it does
nothing, if it accepts the ignoring of its repeated resolutions
calling for the withdrawal of invading forces, then it will have
admitted failure. That failure would be a blow to the authority
and influence of the U.N. in the world, and to the hopes which
humanity placed in the U.N. as the means of achieving peace
with justice.

How timely and pertinent his warnings sound today.

President Eisenhower followed his words with deeds. He made it
unmistakably clear to the Israelis that unless they withdrew their
forces forthwith, all economic and military assistance would be
discontinued. It did not take the Israelis long to heed the message
and to withdraw forthwith.

That was the heyday when the U.N., international law and legal-
ity were the arbiters of disputes and the sanctuary at which the
victims of aggression obtained redress.

But when the Israeli entity today receives annually close to
$6 billion in aid, directly and indirectly through tax-deductible
transfers, syphoned off from the hard-working American taxpayer,
already over-burdened, and when the Israeli military arsenal is
continually swelled by the most sophisticated and massive armaments, it is hardly surprising that they would not be accommodating, even to their greatest benefactor – and much less so to the U.N.
which depends for its effectiveness upon the collective wills of its
members and, particularly, a confluence of the mighty powers.

Lauterpacht in *Recognition in International Law* and McMahon in
Conquest and Modern International Law state: 'The doctrine of non-
recognition is based on the view, that acts contrary to international
law are invalid and cannot become a source of legal rights to the
wrongdoer.' Lauterpacht–Oppenheim's *International Law* further
states: 'After the end of hostilities, there is full room for the application of the principle that no rights and benefits can accrue to the
aggressor from his unlawful act.' Indeed, the second paragraph of
the preamble to resolution 242 emphasizes the inadmissibility of
the acquisition of territory by force, as all U.N. resolutions based
on the Charter have emphasized that all Israeli measures in the
occupied Palestinian and Arab territories have no validity what-

soever; that they are null and void and should be rescinded. Has adherence to the Charter and the recognized principles of international law turned the U.N. into a monstrous sinner in the eyes of the representative of the Israeli entity and its brainwashed supporters? Perhaps the Israelis, by some divine ordinance, regard themselves as above the law which applies only to the rest of us humankind.[27]

The late President Johnson declared in the aftermath of 1967 that the U.S.A. was committed to the survival of Israel but not to its conquests. King Hussein of Jordan has been stating for a whole decade that Israel can have peace *or* territory, but cannot have both. Security Council resolution 242 was categorically emphatic on the inadmissibility of the acquisition of territory by force and called for withdrawal of Israeli forces from the occupied territories in exchange for peace.

Mr Begin's government has declared itself to be openly in defiance of this legal and moral framework by annexing Arab East Jerusalem – having expanded it fifteen-fold to comprise one-fifth of the tiny West Bank by colonizing one-third of the whole of the West Bank and portions of the tiny Gaza Strip and by according itself the sole prerogative of retaining or handing back territory in both Sinai and the Golan Heights. Can this, by any criteria, be anything but forcible conquest, a *diktat*?[20]

Every time the Palestinian question comes to the fore, the Israeli occupiers, like the expert jugglers they are, produce from their rich Pandora's box a multitude of side-issues, so as to avoid confronting the moment of truth and of decision-making. Is that the result of a guilty conscience or of unbridled greed? It is both, notwithstanding their claim and the undiscerning claim of their supporters that it is Israel's survival which they are concerned about.

Can anyone tell me what all those shrill voices of anti-peace mean by 'Israel'? What are its boundaries? What are its limits? Or is it, to repeat the words of General Dayan, the farthest point to which Israeli militarism reaches?

And supposing, for argument's sake, that they strive to occupy half or all of the Middle East, would the supporters of Israel continue to base their argument on the absurd thesis of concern for the survival of Israel? Would those committed to Israel's survival connive at such expansionism in the name of Israel's survival?

The only legal and valid framework for a just and legitimate

settlement is General Assembly resolutions 181, on the establishment of a Palestinian State and of an Israeli State within secure,
defined and recognized boundaries; resolution 194, on the right of
the Palestinian refugees to return to their homeland and live in
peace with their neighbours; and Security Council resolutions 242
and 338, which are general formulations, complementary to the
other valid resolutions.

If the parties directly concerned in the conflict agree or disagree
about altering or amending the existing legal framework through
negotiation and mutual agreement, it is their right and prerogative
to do so. The U.N. can subsequently take cognizance of any mutu-
ally agreed-upon legal framework and, at its discretion, decide
what course of action to take.

After 30 years in exile and over 12 years of occupation and
colonization, there are people who want the Palestinian people to
wait, to give more time for the powers that be to act.

> History is the long and tragic story of the fact that privileged
> groups seldom give up their privileges voluntarily. Individuals
> may see the moral light and voluntarily give up their unjust
> posture. But groups are more immoral than individuals.

There are people who prefer a negative peace, which is the
absence of tension and conflict, to a positive peace, which is the
presence of justice; who constantly say 'I agree with you in the goal
you seek, but I cannot agree with your methods of direct action';
who can paternalistically feel that they can set the timetable for
other people's freedom; who live by the myth of time and constantly advise waiting until a 'more convenient season'. Shallow
understanding from people of good will is more frustrating than no
understanding from people of ill will. Luke-warm acceptance is
much more bewildering than outright rejection.

A good deal of what I have just said has been outright plagiarism, for which I need make no apology. For I have been quoting,
with minor modifications, from one of the great masters of
humanistic thought and action, the inspiring Martin Luther King,
whose *Letter From Birmingham City Jail* (1963) is one of the great
humanistic classics of our time. If anybody wishes to address himself to the plight of the Palestinian people, he could not find a more
logical or profound champion.[39]

The painstaking efforts exerted over the past decades to bring about a peaceful settlement, have been to no avail. The Israeli entity has flouted General Assembly resolution 181, which would have created a Palestinian Arab State and a Jewish State in Palestine. They reneged on the Lausanne Protocol of 12 May 1949, signed by both parties. The Israeli representative's claim that the Arab States had rejected the plan and therefore had no right under it is misleading on two counts:

(1) It was a matter for the Palestinians, in an appropriate form, whether it be a plebiscite or elections, to decide on acceptance or otherwise. This was never done either by U.N. machinery or by the British Mandate authorities. The Palestinians did not have a government to decide on acceptance or declare war. The Palestinians were naturally dismayed at the dismemberment of their country and expressed their disenchantment in speeches, declarations and a few riots and protests immediately after the adoption of the partition plan. But it was the Israeli military machine which seized the opportunity, a few days later, to launch organized, all-out attacks against the wholly disarmed Palestinian people during the mandate. I can very well understand this military machine defending the newly created Jewish State within the boundaries delineated by the General Assembly resolution. But what is totally in violation of the resolution, the Charter and international law is for Israel to have attacked and seized four-fifths of Palestine, including substantial areas earmarked for a Palestine Arab State, even before the British Mandate came to an end, on 15 May 1948.

(2) The contingents from neighbouring Arab countries did not enter Palestine after the end of the mandate to destroy Israel, but simply to save the remnants of the Palestinian people from relentless attacks, massacre and evictions by the Israeli forces.

The British Foreign Secretary of that period, the late Mr Bevin, was given assurances to this effect by the Arab States which had sent limited contingents of their troops for this rescue operation. It is startling that the British Foreign Office which, under the law, releases secret documents after the lapse of 50 years, including hair-raising secrets of world wars and other cataclysmic events, had to request a special Act, a few years ago, to make one and only one single exception to the rule, namely questions relating to Palestine and the Middle East over the past 50 years. The secret wheelings and dealings must have been well below the belt not to allow for publication. The British people and their press are second to none in seeking and exercising freedom of expression. Why are they remaining mute on this ultra-mysterious cover-up?

After 1967, the Israelis strove tirelessly to pre-empt, on the ground, resolutions 242 and 338, adopted unanimously by no less a body than the Security Council, while paying lip service to the said resolution. The Israeli entity declared an official annexation of the whole of Jerusalem and, by on-the-ground colonization, a *de facto* annexation of substantial portions of the occupied Palestinian and Arab lands. The whole world, naturally enough, has categorically rejected these expansionist measures as null and void. But the Israeli entity regards itself as above and beyond international law. For after all, how can humanity compete with alleged divinity? How can a peaceful settlement be achieved under such false and distorted perspectives? Are the Israelis serious in thinking that the Palestinians and the rest of the Arab World would ever agree to capitulate and sign their own demise?

On 15 May 1948, the Law of Return codified the Jewish people's concept of self-promulgation as the State, not of the Israeli people living in the territory, but of Jewish people everywhere. It accords every Jew, of whatever nationality or race, an automatic right to colonize Palestine, while the indigenous Palestinian is committed to squat in refugee camps or roam the world looking for asylum which, in most cases, is denied him.

There is almost universal recognition that the Palestinian people, though in exile, do indeed exist, flesh and blood, and are not phantoms created by the Arab States to serve some mysterious and sinister purpose; the whole world is agreed that Palestinian restoration and redemption is at the core of the Middle East conflict.[27]

Under international law, residual and ultimate sovereignty lies in the Palestinian people, the people who have lived uninterruptedly in the land for thousands of years. Theirs is the ultimate sovereignty over the territory.

The second level of sovereignty, according to the U.N., is inscribed in General Assembly resolutions 181 (II) of 1947 and 194 (III) of 1948, which partitioned Palestine and which would have given to the Palestinians far larger amounts of territory than the Israelis have usurped by force, by terror, by their military machine. That is the only sovereignty recognized by the U.N. I maintain that even Security Council resolutions 242 (1967) and 338 (1973) in no way invalidate the basic, ultimate sovereignty; they in no way change the situation regarding which land belongs to whom. The Security Council resolutions did not drop from the clear blue sky. They did not abrogate the older resolutions which are on the books and which are reconfirmed every year.[33]

8
The West Bank

What exactly have the Israeli occupation authorities perpetrated up to the end of 1978? And beyond?

Israel has expropriated so far, according to my Government's statistics, 1,625,000 dunums of land – a dunum is 1,000 square metres. Israeli statistics concede the confiscation of 1,500,000 dunums. Even accepting Israeli figures, the confiscated lands constitute 27.3% of the total area of the tiny West Bank.

The confiscated lands, buildings and properties comprise the following categories:

(1) The so-called state domains,* which are in fact the communal possession of the various town and village centres which have been utilized by them for countless centuries. Thus, the 60,000 dunums confiscated at Khan-ul-Ahmar, 10 miles from the River Jordan, where the Israeli occupation has constructed an industrial complex with full infrastructure and housing, belong indisputably to the villagers of Eizariyah, Abu Dees and Silwan,

---

*The term 'state domain' is a misnomer. The authentic name is 'public domain', which is the communal possession of the inhabitants in each particular area and was recognized and meticulously delineated as such during the British mandate. Israel deliberately falsified the difference in legal status between the 'Miri' lands and the 'public domain' lands. The Miri lands have over the centuries been individually owned by village- and town-dwellers, but were treated differently in terms of tax-rates. These constitute 1,030,000 dunums out of the total area of the tiny West Bank, a mere 5,500,000 dunums, the equivalent of roughly 3,400 square miles.[48]

suburbs of Jerusalem. It is there that the villagers have been cultivating and grazing for centuries.

(2) Confiscation of the lands and properties of the so-called absentee owners. They are all Palestinian West Bank inhabitants who happened to be outside the country when the June war broke out. They have been denied repatriation to their homes and homeland, and yet the Israelis call them absentees.

(3) Foreclosure and confiscation of lands in the West Bank, even where the owners are present, on the spurious grounds of so-called security and military needs. What security or military needs can be served by depriving a villager from his life-sustaining livelihood is a question which only the Israeli military commanders can answer.

It is noteworthy to recall that, recently, the villagers of Nebi Saleh to the west of Jerusalem, whose lands had been expropriated on the grounds that they did not possess title-deeds, brought action before the Supreme Court, in which they produced documentation and evidence of uninterrupted possession, including tax-payment receipts. When the villagers won the case, the Israeli Government halted the confiscation of other lands on the grounds of validity of possession. All notices of expropriation to the victims have since been based on the grounds of security or military needs, over which courts have no jurisdiction whatsoever.

(4) Forcing the farmers to substitute their lands for more marginal ones, resulting in further land fragmentation, dispersal and flight from the land, to the slave-labour market of the Israeli economy or emigration for the fourth time in a lifetime.

(5) There have been instances of outright forgeries in collusion with the occupation authorities where individuals, who do not own or have any entitlement to a piece of land, have sold it on false pretences. The Arab and Israeli newspapers published several instances of such calculated fraud.

The close to one-third of the West Bank expropriated so far has not spared a single area or location. Upwards of 79 settlements and residential areas colonized by the Israelis – they were 68 up to the end of 1978 – have been constructed on 347,874 dunums of private land, and their breakdown is indicative, beyond any shadow of doubt, of the overall strategy and strategic plans which the Israelis are bent on achieving, time and the availability of sufficient immigrants being the only constraints. Money is evidently abundant from outside countries.

The geographic breakdown of colonization on parts of the 1.5 million dunums of land is as follows:

(1) Jerusalem and its environs: 94,564 dunums. The Israeli settlers in Arab Jerusalem are estimated at 40–50,000 intruders. But numbers – ominous as they are – fail to convey the full tale. By Israeli colonization, Palestinian Arab East Jerusalem, a small portion of the Palestinian Arab Jerusalem of 1948, which included 70% of Western misnamed 'Israeli' Jerusalem, has been expanded fifteen-fold. It presently stretches from the doorsteps of Bethlehem in the south to the twin towns of Ramallah and Bireh in the north – a distance of 40 kilometres.

If this were not enough, Israel's General Sharoon has disclosed his designs to increase Jerusalem's population to one million. Where will this avalanche of people settle? General Sharoon reckons with two possibilities: (a) the compulsive fading away of the 105,000 Palestinian Arab Jerusalemites, weary and exhausted by the strangulation of a ghetto and an unbearable existence, or so he calculates; (b) if East Jerusalem's boundaries have been expanded with impunity to Bethlehem and Ramallah, it should not be impossible to expand them much further to Hebron in the south and to Nablus in the north, incorporating along the way the lands, residential quarters and villages of an ever-depleted and stagnant population. At least this is how Sharoon calculates. Since there is an ever-expanding universe, why not an infinitely expanding Jerusalem? It presently constitutes one-fifth of the entire West Bank.

Racist and religious exclusiveness is best proved by the fact that, after the 1967 war, the Israeli authorities advised that all construction and settlement should not be conducted in the western parts of Jerusalem, which are far more spacious and are already in Israeli control, but in the Palestinian Arab eastern sectors, to achieve the closing of the ring and the choking-off of the Palestinian inhabitants.

(2) Ramallah and Bireh townships: 35,600 dunums upon which 12 settlements have been constructed.

(3) Hebron, Bethlehem and Jericho towns: 116,000 dunums have been colonized on 12 settlements.

(4) Nablus, Tulkarm and Jenin cities: 20,860 dunums have been colonized in 14 settlements. This represents a part of Likud's policy of Israel's creeping expansion from the west into the Palestinian

Arabs' remaining habitat. I shall elaborate later on the strategic plans of both the Labour coalition and the Likud.

(5) The Jordan Valley where 80,700 dunums have been colonized in 19 settlements. I should add here that, but for the town of Jericho and a few adjacent agricultural Palestinian Arab villages such as 'Uojah, the whole of the Jordan Valley in the West Bank from south to north, from Beisan to the Dead Sea, is firmly settled by Israeli colonizers. Not only have they bored deep water-wells, which turned dry or excessively saline the existing Arab wells; they have also been pumping as much water as they need to maximize their exploitation of this fertile off-season valley at the expense of the Palestinian farmers. The Jordan Government's figures indicate that there are already 91,000 Israeli colonizers in Arab Jerusalem, its environs and the rest of the West Bank.

There is another dimension to the plight of our people under occupation which, many believe, goes a long way to explaining one of the ultimate aims of Israeli colonization. (The sickening repetition of 'security grounds' by the Israelis is not even worth replying to.) One of the foremost objectives of Israeli planners is to exploit the water resources of the West Bank, amounting to 895,000,000 cubic metres.

Considering that the consumption of water in the West Bank did not exceed 120,000,000 cubic metres in the year 1977, because of Israeli control of Palestinian wells by installing meters on existing wells, the destruction of others, and the refusal to give any permits for additional drilling, except to the Israeli colonizers, in addition to the stagnation – if not depletion – of the existing population, it will be seen that there remains in the West Bank a substantial surplus of unutilized water, amounting to 630–750,000,000 cubic metres of water fit for irrigation and home consumption, as well as for industrial uses.

The water resources from various sources in the 1948 Israeli-held territories were estimated in 1977 at 1,650,000,000 cubic metres, according to the figures presented by the Israelis to the Desertification Conference, held in Nairobi, Kenya, in September 1977. 36%, or the equivalent of 610,000,000 cubic metres, are procured from Lake Tiberias and the fountainhead of the Yarkun River in Palestine, both of which derive water from the watershed of Syria, the River Jordan and its tributaries.

The confluence runs in two lines across the centre of the country to the south and thence to the Negev at a capacity of 290,000,000 cubic metres per annum. The remaining 64% is derived from water-wells bored in the mountainous regions, the coastal area and other accumulations.

With the manifold increase in the Israeli population, in consequence of vast immigration and expansion of agriculture and industry, occupied Palestine's consumption of water for agriculture, industry and domestic uses has increased from 426,000,000 cubic metres in 1948 to 1,600,000,000 cubic metres in 1977.

Consequently Israel has, since the early 1970s, been consuming all the available water resources. This year [1979], water consumption will approximate 1,820,000,000 cubic metres. In 1985, consumption is expected to reach 2–2.1 billion cubic metres. With an expected deficit of 415–510,000,000 cubic metres, assuming that agricultural consumption remains constant, the Israeli authorities have decided to take the water resources of the West Bank, along with the land and the people.

Next, I shall try to explain the strategic objectives of the policy of settlements and colonization.

(1) There are presently three substantial belts of settlements. The first and one of the earliest ones covers almost the whole of the Jordan Valley, with the aim of cutting off the West Bank's populated areas from any physical contact with East Jordan as contiguous territories. The fact that Palestinians are occasionally allowed to visit their closest kin on the West Bank is a part of the lucrative tourist plans, after the capture of Arab Jerusalem and its holy places, which are presently netting Israel's coffers close to $1 billion per annum. Agricultural exports are permitted in order to prevent them from competing with and beating the highly subsidized Israeli products. This belt of the Jordan Valley is known in political terms as the Allon Line, with its accompanying wire fences, electronic equipment and colonization.

The second belt presently comprises nine agricultural and industrial complexes, the biggest being the Khan-ul-Ahmar industrial town, 10 miles from the River Jordan. These colonies are located on the highlands of the Jordan rift, starting at the Jerusalem–Jericho road and connecting with the first belt of settlements at the West Bank's northern armistice line with Israel. A new, so-called 'Allon-Plan Road' was constructed to connect the colonies on the highlands with those in the Jordan Valley. Large waterpipes are bringing water down the hills to these colonies from the ein Fara water spring which used to supply Jerusalem's water needs. A primary objective of these two belts – apart from sheer colonization and economic exploitation – is to contain the Palestinian population by completing their encirclement from the north, west, south and east by the two belts of colonies.

The third belt of colonization, currently in accelerated implementation by the Likud Government, is the establishment of a chain of colonies along the entire length of the western highlands of the northern, central and southern parts of the West Bank. This is designed to meet the Herut Party's strategic objectives on the West Bank, which Begin never tires of calling the 'liberated territories' as a part of 'greater Israel'. This third belt is moving the former Israeli armistice line right inside the Palestinian populated areas and hinterland. It is also designed to divide the populated areas of the West Bank into smaller areas. The containment of the Palestinians would be facilitated by enclosing them from all sides.

To supplement this plan of control, several lateral highways have been constructed or are under construction to connect 1948 Israel with the three belts. One highway connects Latrun on the Jaffa–Jerusalem road with Qalandia, 15 kilometres from Jerusalem where a 61-industries complex has been constructed. Another, in the southern region of the West Bank, is already open and asphalted halfway to the Dead Sea. A third highway, called the 'Trans-Samarian Highway', would bisect the northern regions of the West Bank and is presently under construction. Another lateral highway further north is still in the planning stage.

On 18 January 1979, Begin's Government allocated some $40 million for expanding and strengthening the settlements and also for constructing power, water, sewage and telephone lines in the third belt of colonies.

As for the high-rise residential fortresses which form a ring around our Holy City of Jerusalem, one of the main objectives is to create in the inhabitants of Jerusalem a psychological feeling of living in a ghetto, in the hope of causing the Palestinians of Jerusalem to emigrate and leave a monolithic Israeli possession of the entire city.

On 29 January 1979, the Israeli Government coalition blocs approved a special draft legislation to compel all foreign embassies to transfer to Jerusalem. We are confident then none will comply with this illegality, the consequences of which would result in a fundamental reappraisal of many countries' relationships with those who may comply, in violation of U.N. solemn resolutions. But Zionist blackmail knows no limits and has no regard for other States' national interests. They have already started a campaign to achieve their end. In the meantime, their desecration of the Haram-Al Shareef area and, particularly, the endless deep diggings below the foundations of the Al-Aqsa Holy Mosque, the first Qibla in Islam, threatens this most sacred sanctuary with eventual collapse, and the process is continuing.

Similarly, the holy sanctuary of Al-Haram Al-Ibrahimi in Hebron, which for 1,400 years has been an Islamic mosque and was never for one day a Jewish synagogue, has to all intents and purposes been transformed into a Jewish synagogue. Almost daily, both night and day, the settlers at Kiryat Arba' and Israelis from other parts of Palestine break into the mosque, molest and shout obscene language at the Muslim worshippers and attendants. During the past two months, an intensified campaign was begun by the Jewish colonizers, under the protection of the occupation authorities, to complete the transformation of this 1,400-year-old mosque into a synagogue and to deny Muslims even the right to worship, especially on Saturdays. The main, spacious prayer court of the mosque has already been occupied. The Head of the Supreme Islamic Council has described the situation as intolerable and has sent an urgent appeal for action.

I have confined my remarks to the all-out colonization of Jerusalem and the rest of the West Bank. Our latest reports indicate that 27 new and additional settlements are being planned, the only impediment to implementation being the lack of people and time. Money is abundant from other nations' taxpayers and from exploitation, as I have already said.

Israeli indulgence in these reprehensible policies mirrors the manner in which the Israelis view the occupied territories and their inhabitants as objects to be exploited, not as human beings whose inherent and inalienable worth must be respected, in spite of their temporary adversity. Even the environment and ecology – God's great creation – are viewed with disrespect and derision.

The Israelis have already drawn up a notorious plan to bring the Mediterranean Sea to cross and inundate regions of the occupied West Bank, downhill to the River Jordan, which is sacred to hundreds of millions, and thence to the Dead Sea for dumping. The Israelis are seriously studying this ecological crime to generate electricity and bring Mediterranean saline waterways and ports to the Jordan Valley.

Does it very much matter to them if, in the process, large areas of the occupied West Bank are laid to waste? If the River Jordan becomes so saline as to be unfit for human, animal and plant? And if the Dead Sea bursts its shores and drowns large areas of the East Bank? It may seem like fantasy or clever engineering. . . but at what cost to the Holy Land and its Palestinian and Jordanian people?

Having outlined the magnitude and manifold aspects of the Israeli aggression, what a pale and futile mockery becomes any talk about 'live and let live', about peace and stability in the Middle East and far beyond, how shallow and meaningless become references to Security Council resolutions or General Assembly resolutions.

Holy Jerusalem will never be alienated from the hundreds of millions who revere it as an integral part of their religious and historical legacy; the Palestinians will never forsake their ancestral homeland. Elementary justice, the rule of law in international relations and a scrupulous observance of Security Council and other U.N. resolutions are the only guarantee of regional, as well as global, peace and security.

What is at stake is nothing less than literally the very survival of the Palestinian people in their homeland and, hence, the possibility or otherwise of achieving a just and lasting peace in the Middle East. There was a time when States were obsessed with the so-called survival of Israel. The time is long overdue when the world should become concerned about Israel's conquests and aggrandizement and be concerned with the fate of the Palestinian people.[30]

Ever since the occupation, Israel has set out to reap what economic benefits it could from the resources of the West Bank. According to available 1977 figures, Israel took about 62% of the West Bank's exports and provided 90% of its imports, while the East Bank provided a market for 37% of the West Bank exports, thus alleviating the suffering and compensating for the lost markets of our people under occupation.

The West Bank trade deficit with Israel is financed simply by its surplus with Jordan and by the remittances of West Bank Palesti-

nian workers abroad. The West Bank, under the present circumstances, offers Israeli industries an almost completely protected
market, which results in the West Bankers paying higher prices for
Israeli goods. How do you expect to have a prosperous economy
when the rate of inflation is 40% or 50% or 60% per annum? Thus,
in short, the West Bank offers Israel a captive market totally
dependent on developments in Israel, and incapable of standing on
its own feet, with restrictive and oftentimes oppressive conditions
under occupation.

Job opportunities on the West Bank itself are on the decline;
obliged to earn a living, West Bankers are forced to seek employment in Israel. Israel is taking advantage of our 60,000 West Bank
workers at far lower wages than those paid to Israeli workers. Most
of the confiscated land set aside for Israeli settlements has been the
best agricultural land on the West Bank. For instance, 80% of
agricultural land on the West Bank of the Jordan Valley has been
confiscated for alleged military purposes. Water resources are
being syphoned off to supply Israeli settlements with their water
needs. While existing artesian wells have been tapped, the Arabs
have been restricted, and no new wells are allowed to be drilled
without prior permission. Almost all such Arab requests have been
'pending' – of course they remain pending – while Israel so far has
drilled scores of new artesian wells on the West Bank to meet the
water needs of its settlements thereon, in addition to taking over
substantial amounts of existing Palestinian water, springs and
wells. Even the philanthropic project of Al-Mashru' al-Inshaai of
Musa Alami, in Jericho, which had 20 wells and which is of international renown, had 18 of its 20 wells destroyed. This has resulted
in adjacent Arab wells being depleted and drying up, in many
cases.

The conditions of hardship for Palestinians in the West Bank
created by the Israeli occupation authorities are best summed up
by the accelerating change in the geographic, demographic,
economic and, above all, the historical, cultural and religious legacy dramatized by the continuing tragedy in our Holy Jerusalem,
which is far more precious to us than all the gold in the world. This
has aggravated the internal haemorrhage of the occupied Arab
territories. Apart from continued deportation of West Bankers
since 1967, conditions in the West Bank, last year alone, forced
some 22,000 persons to cross to the East Bank of Jordan. In 1968 I

was Minister of Reconstruction in the Jordan Government, and we had to cater to almost 300,000 displaced persons from the West Bank and the Gaza Strip. And I am not talking about the 1.75 million refugees who have been literally sleeping under the skies and on the ground for 30 years while the Israelis have been living in their furnished homes.

With increasing settlement of the West Bank by Israelis, one wonders what would stop Israel forcing more and more Arabs out of the West Bank, in its various devious ways, in the event of the proposed bilateral peace treaty taking effect. Such an exodus would further swell the ranks of the hundreds of thousands of embittered refugees, embodying the contradiction that Israel presents, claiming to fear radicalism, while itself creating and exporting that very brand of bitterness that it claims to fear.

There is a fundamental conceptual difference between (a) the so-called autonomy on the West Bank established on the ground to achieve a *fait accompli* and (b) the *status quo* and the implementation of U.N. Security Council resolutions 242 and 338 in addition, of course, to the previous resolutions relative to the *status quo ante*. The Accords and the proposed peace treaty have not halted the major changes in the occupied territories, nor will the ensuing period alter the facts created by the occupation. The purported 'autonomy' envisaged by the Accord process subjects the occupied territories to a clear separation of the Palestinian people, their rights and their political future, from the land, from their links to the land and its resources, which can only in harmony represent the life, the vitality, of the West Bank. The incontrovertible fact today is that the mood of the area is smitten with unprecedented doubts and fears about the future and the stability of the Middle East, in consequence of the planned abandonment and the eventual obliteration of the Palestinian people.[33]

The latest Israeli inhuman practices in the occupied West Bank of Jordan not only defy the principles of the Charter of the U.N. but also violate the principles of the Fourth Geneva Convention of 1949 relating to the protection of civilians under occupation, to which Israel is a signatory.

(1) On 4 June 1979, Israeli occupation authorities demolished the home of —— in the town of Al-Jariah, near Ramallah. She was accused of resisting Israeli occupation. Four other houses were sealed off and their owners arrested on the pretext of resisting

Israeli occupation. The first house, in the area of Ramallah, was owned by an Arab girl. The second house, in the town of Al-Bireh, was owned by another Arab girl. The other two houses, also in Al-Bireh, were owned by ——.

(2) On 3 June 1979, the Arab inhabitants of Silwan, near Jerusalem, sent Prime Minister Begin a message protesting the expropriation of more than 100,000 dunums of their cultivated land in the area of Maale Adumin (Al-Khan Al-Ahmar) near Jericho, and in the Dead Sea area. This land is the only source of their livelihood and that of Silwan. They told Begin to send a copy of their message to President Carter and Egypt's President, Anwar Sadat.

(3) On 3 June 1979, Israel's Cabinet approved the establishment of a Jewish settlement named Elon Moreh on several thousands of dunums of privately owned Arab land, in the area of the village of Rujib, seven kilometres south of Nablus. The Gush Emunim group, the henchmen of Begin, are planning an urban Jewish centre of about 100,000 Israeli settlers – twice as large as the Arab city of Nablus.

(4) On 7 June 1979, the Israeli newspaper *Ma'ariv* reported that the Gush Emunim gang is leading a large and vicious campaign for expanding the land areas of existing Jewish settlements in the West Bank of Jordan. The following list shows the present area of each settlement in dunums and the planned expansion of each one of them:

	Present area	Required area
Dotan (Sanur)	46	1,500
Shomron	100	1,500
Qaddum	300	1,500
Qarney – Shomron	150	1,500
El-Qana	310	1,500
Ariail	110	5,000
Tapuah	150	1,500
Neve Zuf	900	1,500
Ofra	350	1,500
Beit El	225	1,500
Beit Horon	150	1,500
Giv'on	90	5,000
Mizpeh Jericho	1,000	1,500
Qiryat Arba	4,250	5,000

Hours after the Israeli Cabinet approved the establishment of the Elon Moreh settlement near Nablus, Begin said: 'There has never been an action more legal than settlement by Jews in all the territories of the land of Israel.' Given the Zionist character of Israel and its shameless record since its creation in 1948, there can never be a greater insult to the values of mankind than Begin's statement.[36]

On 22 March 1979 the Security Council adopted resolution 446, establishing a Commission whose mandate was 'to examine the situation relating to settlements in the Arab territories, occupied since 1967, including Jerusalem'. The Commission submitted its first report, after an intensive study of the situation in the area, on 12 July 1979. The culpable party against which the complaint had been made and whose criminal aggression against the Palestinian and Arab peoples posed a present, continuing and grave danger not only to international law and elemental justice but, in equal measure, to international peace and security, refused even to accord the Security Council Commission entry into the occupied territories, let alone to concede to the Security Council any jurisdiction in the matter, coupled with an *a priori* rejection of its findings.

On 15 February 1980, Israel's Ambassador-designate to Egypt and a top confidant of Menachem Begin, echoing his master's voice, publicly denounced the U.S. Government for its appeals to Israel to curb Jewish settlements in the occupied territories. 'I deny any right to any foreign power to intervene in our policy of settlement,' declared Ben Elissar at a news conference. This associate of Begin called the right of settlement: 'a basic inherent right that is denied only by those who want to see us back to the lines of 1967'.

By the spring of 1979, the Israeli occupation had confiscated 27.1% of the occupied West Bank, including Jerusalem. In the intervening year, the floodgates of colonization have burst into a devastating and uncontrollable avalanche. During the April–October 1979 period alone, Israel confiscated an additional 230,000 dunums of Arab lands, thus increasing the total area seized to 1,730,000 dunums, which accounts for about 31.4% of the total area of the West Bank. Thus, in a period of only six months, the total area seized increased by 15%.

Although no exact data exist for the total number of Israeli colonizers in Israel's ever-accelerating expansion the total number of settlers has significantly increased beyond the 91,000 figure reported for April 1979. The colonizers are housed in 87 illegal settlements of which 18 were in or around Jerusalem, 22 in the Jordan Valley and the rest entrenched in every corner and location throughout the length and breadth of the occupied West Bank, including cities, towns and villages.

Only recently, the people of Jerusalem were watching Israeli bulldozers opening 30-metre-wide roads for a town which is being built at the last relatively open entrance to Jerusalem from the east, adjacent to and on lands confiscated from the villagers of Eizeriyah, overlooking Bethany and a few kilometres from the centre of Arab Jerusalem.

The construction of this town (named Ma'alet Adomim) completes the closing of the ring around Arab Jerusalem, already cut off from the rest of the world by massive Israeli colonization in the north up to Ramallah, from the south up to the town of Bethlehem, and to the west by Israel's usurpation of two-thirds of Palestinian West Jerusalem in 1948, cutting it off from the Mediterranean Sea, and a long stretch of Israeli colonization along the western mountain ranges all the way from Bethlehem to Ramallah.

Now, to give just random examples, here are reports of Israeli colonization running berserk.

The Israeli occupation authorities have confiscated 2,500 dunums of land belonging to the two Arab villages of al-Khader and Beit Ummar to the east of the Bethlehem road near Wadi-al Bayyar. Two days earlier, the occupation authorities celebrated the laying-down of the cornerstone for a new town to be named Ifrat on the lands of the two villages. The new town, located between occupied Jerusalem and the Kfar Etzion complex, will consist of 5,000 housing units. New Jewish citizens from New York and South Africa will be settled in this town.

To the north of the West Bank, the cornerstone will be laid for the construction of Carti Shamroon No. 2 in the mountain city of Nablus. Mr Sakhr Abu Ayyash, speaking for the dispossessed villagers of Beit Ummar, declared: 'At the time when we have been demanding the removal of the earlier settlement Majdal Ouz on our land, we find ourselves faced with the construction of yet another one.'

On 14 February this year, the occupation authorities confiscated an additional 1,000 dunums of land belonging to the village of Abboud to the north-east of Ramallah, in order to build a new settlement, to be named Levota. This is at an equal-distance between north and south to ensure that the inimical and ubiquitous colonization is fairly equally shared.

The total picture is gruesome indeed, the more so as it is part and parcel of an overall and inexorable process spelt out not only in our reports but in a notorious official Israeli document which has the approval of Begin and his party. Furthermore, it is being sytematically implemented on the ground literally as laid down on paper. It is known as the 'Master Plan for the Development of Settlements in Judea and Samaria' and its author is Matityaho Drobles; it covers the period 1979–83. This colonization plan was issued by the Department for Rural Settlements at the World Zionist Organization in a triangular affiliation with the Israeli nation and the Jewish Agency.

The plan determines the establishment of 46 new settlements over its lifespan, to be inhabited by 16,000 families. The cost of the plan is £132 billion, that is in excess of $2.5 billion. Furthermore, the plan includes the enlarging of 38 existing settlements as well as those under construction at a cost of another £122 billion. Altogether, the plan calls for an additional 27,000 families by the end of 1983, at a cost of £154 billion. The average cost of settling a family is £12 million.

These expenditures and settlements are designed as an initial step in a much more massive colonization of the densely populated highlands of the West Bank. They do not include the other 20-year plan from 1975-95 for the Jordan Valley which is presently under implementation. Even though the Israeli occupation authorities had already seized 80–90% of the Jordan Valley, they have already intensified a colonization plan to encircle that remnant which is still in Palestinian hands, and particularly around the historic city of Jericho, by six new colonies. They will be named Ni'mah (A), Ni'mah (B), Ni'mah (C) – the Israelis seem to be running out of names – and also al-Mog (B), Beit Ha'reh and Matzbeh Yerihu B (Arihah is Jericho's Arabic name). It is established that in January 1979 the Israelis built a colony named Ni'ma to the north of Jericho and the big Palestinian village of 'Uoja.

This is the pattern and motive for encircling every city, town and village complex throughout the whole of the West Bank, as well as dividing them up by establishing settlements between them, as we shall see in a brief analysis of the Drobles Master Plan. The plan is the official plan of the Israeli Government, its Bible.

It is pertinent to highlight a number of significant components in the Israeli entity's official policy of colonization as spelled out in the Master Plan.

(1) It is regarded by the Israelis themselves as just one further step towards taking over the whole of the occupied territories including Jerusalem, which has suffered most by total encirclement and massive colonization. Evidently, as the Report clearly states, after the initial master plan a comprehensive and systematic land survey will take place. When the survey is completed, the Plan adds, it is probable that Israel will be able to plan the disposition of settlements additional to those proposed in the Master Plan.

(2) Settlement throughout the land of Israel, including, according to the Zionists the occupied territories, is for security and as of right. A strip of settlements at strategic sites enhances both internal and external security, as well as making concrete and realizing our right to Eretz Israel.

(3) The disposition of the proposed settlements will take the form of interrelated and integrated blocs or community settlements which will, in the course of time, be turned into urban centres.

(4) The settlements must be carried out not only *around* what it describes as the settlement of the minorities – meaning the Palestinians – but also *in between them*, this in accordance with the settlement policy adopted in Galilee. (This has prompted an outside observer's comment that if this is the way Israel looks to those who, according to law, are its citizens, is it any wonder that the military government is treating the population under occupation in this manner?)

The population of Jerusalem and the West Bank has dwindled by 32% since 1967. Over the past 13 years of occupation, it is a stagnant 600–700,000. If there had been no prolonged occupation, the return of the displaced, of those working abroad whose home is in the West Bank, and their offspring, the natural increase by economic and social development would have raised the population to at least 1.5 million. And yet the ratio of the displaced, the exiles, the so-called absentees is increasing alarmingly as days, months and years go by.

In a report which details Israeli settlement activities covering the period March 1979–January 1980, 11 new settlements have been established, namely

(1) Sal'it on lands confiscated from the village of Kofr Sur to the north of Qalqilia;

(2) the Allon-Moreh settlement five kilometres from Nablus (as a result of a court ruling, a substitute settlement on one of the adjacent hills belonging to the village of Dair-al-Hattab is being constructed);

(3) Kernai Shamroon, on the main road between Nablus and Tulkarm, three kilometres from the earlier established settlement Kernai Shamroon (A) (these are in the third belt previously referred to as advancing from the armistice line of 1967 from the west to the east);

(4) Nevi Tusv, located between the two Arab villages of Dair Ballout and the village of Aaboud to the north of Ramallah in the centre of the West Bank;

(5) Kernai Shamroon (D) to the south of the earlier Kernai Shamroon (A);

(6) Dothan, to the south of the city of Jenin near the town of Ya'bud;

(7) Reehan, near the armistice line in the Jenin district;

(8) Kernai Shamroon (C), eight kilometres from Kernai Shamroon (A);

(9) Elazar settlement in the Kfar Etzion complex on the main road to Hebron;

(10) Ifrat settlement or town on confiscated lands belonging to the village of al-Khader (St George) to the west of Bethlehem;

(11) Jiffa Hadasha, on confiscated lands belonging to the village of al-Jeeb, in the Ramallah district.

Five settlements have been augmented: Ariel Harris in Khofr-Haris-Silfit in the Nablus area; Jiboan on the village lands of al-Jeeb in the Ramallah district; al-Kharja, in the area of Abu Qarnein village; Beit Huron on lands of al-Petra village in the Ramallah district; and the settlement of Afra on lands confiscated from Hawd al-Marja, to the north of Ramallah.

During the past six months, the Israeli occupation authorities confiscated 196,767 dunums. Their locations are in the Khan-el-Ahmar–Dead Sea area, Jenin, Nablus, Hebron, Tulkarm, Bethlehem and Ramallah. I might add the confiscations in and around Jerusalem as well as the confiscation over the years of upwards of

80,000 dunums belonging to the village of Taubass between Nablus and the Jordan Valley in the north.[48]

The facts of the case are as simple as they are awesome. Subsequent to Security Council resolutions 446 and 452 which had forcefully warned Israel of the disastrous consequences of its colonization policy, the occupation authorities went ahead full-speed in confiscating additional lands and water, thereby augmenting their seizures to a stunning 1,700,000 dunums in Jerusalem and the West Bank alone, out of a total area of 5.5 million dunums. That makes an Israeli confiscation of almost one-third of the tiny remnants of the Palestinian homeland.[49]

Jordan urges the Security Council to agree on three steps which are consonant with its own resolutions and solemn responsibilities and should, therefore, be acceptable.

(1) Resolve that an immediate moratorium be imposed, and meticulously observed by the Israeli occupation authorities, over further Israeli colonization and expropriation of Palestinian and other occupied Arab lands. This should be done through an already existing U.N. presence in the Old Government House in occupied Jerusalem, which can be augmented with day-to-day monitoring and reporting, to ensure compliance with the resolution of the Security Council. This would be just a preliminary first-aid effort to stop the blood-letting. We must emphasize within this context that the occupied territories have no 'protecting State' and are totally at the whim of the occupation authority.

(2) The Security Council should send a five-member commission from among its membership to investigate the situation on the spot and to report back to the Council, not later than 1 May, the authenticity or otherwise of our complaint. No courts, national or international, worth their name should shy away from at least investigating a very grave and genuine complaint by an aggrieved party gripped with alarm over its very survival.

(3) If the findings of the Security Council Commission should confirm the authenticity and substance of the complaint, it becomes logically inescapable that the Security Council should exercise the powers vested in it by the Charter, including Chapter VII, to ensure compliance.

I am certain that one day the Security Council will have to face up to this most alarming problem, but under conditions more dangerous and sanguine. Perhaps a timely intervention now would be preferable to such an eventuality. Besides, is it not the responsibility of the Security Council to implement resolutions 242 and 338 and other U.N. resolutions in all their aspects? What has come of that? Or are we to assume that there is an omnipotent, invisible power – it is becoming more visible every day – which carries more weight than the collective power and wills of the highest executive organ of the U.N.?[30]

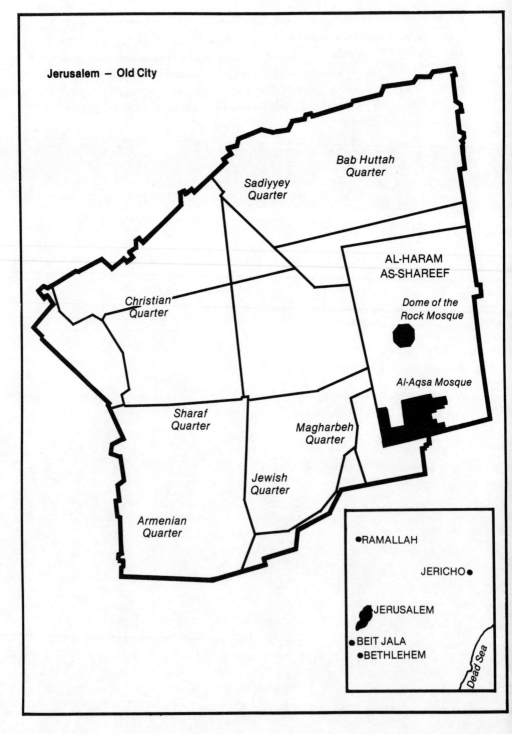

Jerusalem – Old City

9
Jerusalem

Let me describe for you a one-page advertisement issued by the Israel Government Tourist Office in New York and carried by the *New York Times* Magazine of 13 March 1977, by *Time* Magazine of 14 March 1977, and by heaven knows how many other nationally read publications. The whole city of Jerusalem, both old and new, is dwarfed and cramped, with one monument dominating the panorama; parallel to it, stuck to the wall encompassing the monument and almost equal in proportion to it is the name 'ISRAEL' in big capital letters. There is no name or identification of the monument in the advertisement. The only thing in writing describing the area is: '. . .And, finally, you will feel the spiritual beauty of Israel when you enter Jerusalem. A city so ancient, it would still seem like home to David and Solomon.' Is this plagiarism, downright distortion; or something more ominous? I can well understand an Israeli government advertisement giving pride of place to the Knesset or even to the Wailing Wall. But to select the first Qibla of Islam, the Noble Sanctuary, the Dome of the Rock, in the Haram as-Shareef sanctuary as representing Israel is a new peak of distortive misinformation.

The Mosque of the Dome of the Rock has been for over 1,300 years a pivotal centre of Islamic devotion. It is as magnificent a monument to the glory of God (as one Western writer has rightly described it) as can be seen anywhere in the world. It was built in the reign of the Umayyad Caliph Abdul Malik ibn Marwan in the seventh century A.D., and a substantial portion of Egypt's revenues for seven years was spent on its construction and embellishment. Generation after generation of craftsmen, artists and calligraphers painstakingly spent countless years, skills and revenues from the reign of the Umayyads for 1,400 years, the last rejuvenation being undertaken by the Government of Jordan, financed by the Government of the late King Faisal of Saudi Arabia and completed in 1964.[9]

The city of Jerusalem has throughout recorded history been a focal point of international attention, contention and conflict. Its international dimensions, however, have frequently been a source of affliction and suffering rather than a blessing to its indigenous and lawful inhabitants. This has been the fate of Jerusalem in ancient and medieval times, as well as in the contemporary era.

The factors causing Jerusalem's unique position in world affairs are varied: in ancient times, the overriding considerations must have been its pivotal geographic and strategic location astride three continents. The Jebusite Arabs, kinsmen of the highly cultured Canaanites, founded the city of Jerusalem, according to currently available archaeological remains, almost 5,000 years ago during the Bronze Age and named it Uri-Salem, the city of peace. Among the discoveries of the 4,500-year-old city of Ebla, a few years ago, its name on the clay inscriptions is Uru Salema.

The continuing encounters between the powers and empires of those ancient times, first Near Eastern and, later, Mediterranean, inevitably brought them into collision in and around Jerusalem, for control of Jerusalem was the key to the control of a united Palestine, because it is situated on the central ridge which is the most convenient route north and south through the hill country, and an important land route through Asia Minor.

However, the Jebusite Arab and Canaanite inhabitants remained firmly the occupants of Jerusalem and the rest of Palestine. The Philistines, known as the 'people of the sea', came next and settled almost the whole of the coastline of Palestine, 'Philistia', as well as other disparate areas in the hinterland. The Philistines were similarly highly advanced, as is proved by the excavation of pottery, handicrafts and tools with which they handled their lives in peace as in war.

Some time in the period of the twelfth to thirteenth century B.C.,

Hebrew tribesmen of almost no culture at all, as the lack of archaeological finds definitively proves, started their infiltration into Palestine in relatively small groups. Unlike their historical records which were written at various periods generations later and given religious sanctification, the historical truth is that their intrusion and infiltration came from two areas: one from Egypt, and the other from the east across the River Jordan where there are evidences of their destruction of Jericho and other thriving towns. As for those waves which marauded via the Sinai, it has been historically established that they never succeeded in seizing an inch of territory from the formidable Philistines; on the contrary, history tells us that even during their short-lived 70-year kingdom when the Israelites unified the hilly regions of Jerusalem, Nablus and Hebron, they were, in spite of their increased power, virtual satellites of the Philistines. As for the Canaanites and their offshoot in Jerusalem, the Jebusites, they continued to live in their cities, towns and villages, side by side with the Israelite intruders.

The control of Jerusalem by David, dated by historians to be in the year 922 B.C., and his establishment of a largely garrison presence emboldened him towards a policy of military expansion. Though he never succeeded in annexing the Palestine coast or including it in the Israeli domain, he attacked the other neighbouring ancient enemies, Moab, Ammon, Edom and, most striking of all, the Aramaeans, and annexed Damascus. Thus, the Israelites gained military control of large areas of land extending from the Euphrates to the borders of Egypt, although the Phoenician towns along the Syrian coast and the Palestine coast remained impregnable.

The unification of the West Bank with Jerusalem as its capital and centre and expansion beyond enabled the Israelites under David to start learning from the far superior civilizations of the indigenous inhabitants, including their religious experiences, a process considerably accelerated under Solomon. (The Israelites, since ancient times, have always been experts at usurping other people's culture and claiming it for themselves.)

I do not wish to delve too deeply into ancient history; my references to historical and archaeological records are merely intended to lay bare Israel's claims and designs, not only against Jerusalem, but also against the entire Arab region. This is because all Israeli claims are based on purely nationalist religious exclusiveness and short-lived, ephemeral conquest more than 3,000 years ago:

(1) They claim Jerusalem and the rest of the Holy Land as theirs and theirs alone. They evidently want to accomplish far more than their ancient ancestors claimed or succeeded in accomplishing.

(2) They allege that Jerusalem was founded by David, even though history proves beyond any shadow of doubt that it was founded and inhabited uninterruptedly by the Jebusite Semitic Arabs. The Israelis never even conquered it from the outside; they consolidated their stage-by-stage infiltration from within.

(3) An Israeli claim which poses a fundamental spiritual and religious challenge to the entire Islamic faith stems from Israel's unalterable determination to rebuild Solomon's Temple, which was originally built during the tenth century B.C. on a site which the Israelis believe lies beneath the Haram as-Shareef Islamic holy sanctuary, in the centre of which is the Dome of the Rock. They believe the Rock to have been the site of the altar of sacrifices. The existing enclosure, originally Roman, was begun in 19 B.C. by Herod's rebuilding of the Temple. The great walls of the Haram as-Shareef holy sanctuary and of the old City were rebuilt several times by successive Islamic empires, the last being the Ottoman Empire's Sultan Sulayman the Magnificent.

When the Islamic Arab conquests took place in the seventh century A.D. and the Roman Empire was vanquished, there was neither a Temple nor a Jewish presence of any significance. The two temples had been destroyed by both the Babylonians and the Romans, and they had taken the Jews into captivity as well.

It should be stressed at this point that the Islamic Arab conquests were not really conquests of other people's lands but simply a restoration of Arab authority, under the banner of Islam, over territories and peoples of the same Arab race, and the overthrow of an alien empire. The conquests were the last though the greatest of the Arab migrations from the Arabian peninsula to the more fertile lands of Syria, Iraq, Egypt and beyond.

Then came the four major crusades beginning in 1095, and ending in the early part of the fourteenth century. Although masquerading under the name of religion, contemporary historians are predominantly in agreement that the crusades were basically prompted by worldly ambitions. Europe had been living in a state of backwardness and feudalism of social and economic inequities which the Europeans themselves refer to as the Dark Ages. Steeped in ignorance, stagnation and insufferable internal exploitation, Europe's leadership became aware of the Islamic Empire's fabulous wealth, culture, civilization and the great strides which were being achieved in all fields of knowledge and learning. The heartland of that Empire, geographically and spiritually, though not its capital or seat of power, was Jerusalem. The leaders of Europe, in command of vast multitudes of under-utilized manpower, found the prospect of attacking and seizing the incomparably more advanced and prosperous Islamic domains almost irresistible. The ignorant European masses had to be motivated to action by slogans and a cause, no matter how ill-conceived. It was a tragedy of the greatest magnitude that the cause should be a trumped-up hostility towards Islam which, both religiously and traditionally, held Christianity in the greatest veneration and esteem. The residues of that hostility lingered long after the conflict had been ended honourably and magnanimously by the victorious Salah-uddin. (General Allenby went so far as to declare that he had at last settled scores and ended the crusades when he accepted the keys of the city, upon entering Jerusalem in 1917.)

I have mentioned the crusades in this narrative because Jerusalem was the focal point of that prolonged international conflict which, in the guise of recovering Jerusalem from the 'Muslim infidels', sought by capturing it to possess a key gateway to a far larger conquest of the world of Islam in the Near East. For the European invaders did not stop at Jerusalem; they continued their expansion to the point of cutting off the pilgrimage routes to Mecca and Medina at Karak, Ma'aan and other key locations in Jordan. Jerusalem and Palestine have always been a gateway to the conquest of all the other Islamic and Arab domains beyond. Conquerors may differ, but the geopolitical dimensions of Jerusalem and Palestine have been, and will continue to be, unalterable and constant.

As the European continent surged forward in industrialization and progress from the eighteenth century onward, the domains of Islam fell deeper and deeper into the abyss of retrogression and stagnation, and Europe renewed its hostile designs against the domains of Islam: colonialism and imperialism were let loose in fierce rivalry between the European powers. Initially, Jerusalem and Palestine were not the focal point, as in the past. The reasons were twofold: (a) the feuding European powers could only grab them by dismantling the Ottoman Empire which, though in continuing decline, was still sufficiently strong to mobilize the Muslim masses and force a would-be aggressor to think twice before committing himself. Sultan Abdul Hamid's shrewd diplomacy, playing off one European power against another and threatening to declare a holy war, advised against rash adventure. Nor was technological disparity as sharp then as it is today; (b) the European powers themselves were fearful of the disintegration of the Ottoman Empire because they were in deep disagreement as to the division of the spoils.

The British Mandate over Palestine was specifically designed to establish a Jewish national home by all possible means. Under the Treaty of Lausanne of 1923, Turkey was divested of all rights to its sovereignty over Palestine. The mere fact that the mandate to administer Palestine had been given to Britain by the League of Nations did not convey sovereignty to her. Palestine's provisional independence had been recognized with its overwhelming Arab majority.

Politically, economically, militarily and administratively, the story is all too recent, all too well known, to need any lengthy recounting. The Arab–Jewish battle for the control of Jerusalem and Palestine began and intensified during the Mandate.

However, let us examine from a juridical perspective the falsity of the Jewish claims against the Islamic holiest place in Jerusalem, namely the Haram as-Shareef area and the area of the Western Wall 'Al-Buraq' which the Israelis claim to be the Wailing Wall and the site of the ancient Temples. The acid test came in the 1929 Palestinian Arab rebellion known as Thawrat al-Buraq.

During the first decade of the British Mandate, the Government in Jerusalem, guided from London, assumed responsibility for maintaining the *status quo* which had existed during the Ottoman Empire. Repeated attempts were made by the Jews to change the *status quo* by introducing appurtenances of worship not permitted hitherto. Following these attempts, in September 1925 the Government issued a decree banning the Jews from bringing benches, seats and other items to the Wailing Wall. However, on the Day of Atonement in September 1928, the Jews introduced a screen, contrary to that decree, and a British police officer promptly removed it. As usual, the Jews in Palestine and the World Zionist Council raised a malicious campaign in the name of religion, even though it was well established that the Muslims were the legal owners of both the Wall and the pavement in front of it.

Ever since the statements of Weizman in 1918 and of the Chief Rabbi, Kuk, in 1920 demanding the handing over of the Wall as 'the possession of the Jews throughout the world', the Muslim Supreme Council were convinced that the Jews were after possession of the Western Wall of the al-Aqsa Mosque, al-Buraq.

Hundreds of paramilitary Hagana and other youth organizations marched towards the Wailing Wall and hoisted the Zionist flag there. At the urging of their leadership the Arab inhabitants exercised utmost self-restraint, but on the following day, Friday, which coincided with the birthday of the Prophet, counter-demonstrations erupted, and on 23 August widespread disturbances broke out. The Government immediately reaffirmed the terms of the 1928 White Paper maintaining the original *status quo*.

An international commission under the chairmanship of a former Swedish Minister of Foreign Affairs was quickly appointed and approved by the Council of the League of Nations. In December 1930, following the British legal system and after an exhaustive study of documents and evidence, the Commission reached a unanimous verdict as follows:

(1) To the Muslims belong the sole ownership of, and the sole proprietary right to, the Western Wall, as an integral part of Al-Haram as-Shareef area.

(2) To the Muslims also belongs the pavement in front of the Wall and of the adjacent Magharba (Moroccan) quarter, opposite, which was made Waqf under Muslim Shari'a law, dedicated to charitable purposes.

(3) The Jews should have free access to the Western Wall for the purpose of worship, at all times – subject to certain provisions.

It is significant that, after 12 years of digging, the Israelis did not find a trace of their alleged claims against the Haram as-Shareef Sanctuary. The finds were predominantly Islamic, including a huge Umayyad palace, adjacent to the southern wall of al-Aqsa Mosque. There were a few Roman and a few Crusader remains, but none Jewish. The Israelis can usurp history in their writings; but they cannot invent an Israeli presence when it does not exist.

The legal situation in Jerusalem during the British Mandate and up to its termination in 1948 remained static except whenever various proposals for the partition of Palestine, such as the Peel Commission's Plan of 1937, were formulated. The MacDonald White Paper of 1939, however, described partition as 'impracticable' and called for a single State, with an Arab majority. Jerusalem was to be the capital. This remained official British policy until the end of World War II.

The U.N. having inherited the correspondence of the Charter concerning 'mandates' of the League Covenant, began to consider the issue of the future of Palestine in 1947.

In 1946 an Anglo-American Commission was sent to Palestine and its major recommendation was that 100,000 Jewish immigrants be allowed into Palestine from the post-World War II refugee camps. The Palestinian Arabs vehemently objected since it was a further threat to their existence and a violation of the White Paper of 1939, acknowledging Palestine's independence after a five-year interim period. This was followed by the General Assembly's setting up of a Special Committee to determine the future government of Palestine, known as U.N.S.C.O.P. At the request of the Mandatory Power, the General Assembly held a special session and on 29 November 1947 recommended a resolution to partition Palestine into two States, one Palestinian Arab and one Jewish, with an economic union. The minority report was against partition and proposed a federal State. Under the partition plan, a special international regime for the City of Jerusalem was set out in Part III of the plan which should be created two months after the evacuation of the armed forces of the Mandatory Power had been completed but in any case not later than October 1948. During the transition and the establishment of the Provisional Council of Government of each State, each authority would have full control over all matters including immigration and land ownership, no additional Jew should be permitted to establish residence in the area of the proposed Arab State, and no additonal Arab in the proposed Jewish State. But I must emphasize that, whereas the proposed Arab State had a mere 15–20,000 Jews, the proposed Jewish State had almost as many Arabs as Jews.

Even though the plan was rejected by the Arabs and nominally accepted by the Jewish Agency, the Security Council was entrusted to see to it that the plan would be implemented. However, the resolution was never applied and the Jewish forces occupied four-fifths of Palestine, in flagrant violation of the U.N. resolution, and after 1967 they occupied the whole country and beyond.

Regardless of how one views that plan, studying its provisions and wording, with its specific safeguards for the rights on lands, people, religious and historic sites and the recognizable principles of international law, it showed, at least, some sense of respect for basic human and legal rights. In Part III of the partition plan, the city of Jerusalem was to be established as a *corpus separatum* under a special international regime, to be administered by the U.N. According to the plan the boundaries of the city were to include the then present municipality of Jerusalem, plus the surrounding villages and towns, the most eastern of which was Abu Dis, the most southern, Bethlehem, the most western, Ein Karim (including also the built-up areas of Motsa), and the most northern Shu'fat.

The Administering Authority was to pursue the following special objective: to protect and preserve the unique spiritual and religious interests of the three great monotheistic faiths located in the city: to this end, to ensure that order and peace, and especially religious peace, reign in Jerusalem. A governor of the city of Jerusalem was to be appointed, to be selected on the basis of special qualifications and without regard to nationality, but not, however, to be a citizen of either State in Palestine. He was to conduct all powers of administration, including external affairs. Simultaneously, the existing local autonomous units in the territory of the city, namely villages, townships and municipalities, were to enjoy wide powers of local government and administration. Special town units or zones, consisting respectively of the Arab and Jewish sections of new Jerusalem, were to be formed, while continuing to form part of the municipality of Jerusalem. Jerusalem was to have been demilitarized and its neutrality declared and preserved. Chief Justice Fitzgerald had meticulously drawn up the Arab and Jewish zones, and special provision was made for the protection of all Holy Places.

The U.N. failed to implement the plan and the positions of both the Arabs and the Jews changed many times. Count Folke Bernadotte was assassinated by the Jews in Jerusalem for proposing that Jerusalem should be Arab, in his mission to continue the work of the Palestine Conciliation Commission.

The Conciliation Commission, meeting at Lausanne in May 1949, obtained the approval of the Arab States and Israel on implementing the U.N. resolutions, including those on Jerusalem, in a Protocol initialled by both sides. But the Israelis reneged and refused to ratify it, even before the collapse of the conciliation efforts.

On 2 August, claiming a failure by the U.N. to provide a legal framework for Jerusalem, the Israeli authorities declared western Jerusalem to be Israeli-occupied territory (retroactive to 15 May) and started moving its ministries to the Holy City. On 2 August, the military government was disbanded and western Jerusalem annexed.

On 3 April 1949, an Armistice Agreement was signed. Article VIII of the Armistice deals with Jerusalem and calls for a Special Committee to direct its attention, among other matters, to free movement of traffic on vital roads, the return of the Arab citizens of West Jerusalem to their homes, the restoration of public services such as the water of Ras-ul Ein and electricity, in exchange for free access to the Holy Places and cultural institutions and use of the cemetery on the Mount of Olives. The Israelis who have mischievously been misleading the world for 30 years, claiming that Jordan had barred them from visiting the Wailing Wall, conveniently forget that it was they who refused to permit the return of the Arab inhabitants to their homes or the re-opening of vital roads such as the Jerusalem–Bethlehem road or the restoration of the vital supplies of water and electricity to Arab Jerusalem. They preferred the seizure of Arab quarters and homes to visiting what they claim to be their holiest of holies, the Wailing Wall. On every possible occasion they shed crocodile tears over their prohibition from visiting the Wailing Wall between 1948 and 1967, while unabashedly ignoring the other part of the equation regarding Arab rights.

By 1950 it became apparent that internationalization was lacking support, even in the U.N. and, by 1952, the idea was dead. The *de facto status quo* had been practically accepted, although nominally it continued to be observed, even up to 1979.

In 1967, Israeli aggression resulted in the occupation of Arab Jerusalem and the West Bank. Israel immediately began what they called reunification – meaning annexation of Arab Jerusalem. Dayan's first order was the removal of all barriers between the two halves of the city. On 27 June 1967, the Knesset added a paragraph to the so-called Law and Administration Ordinance of 1948 stating:

The State's laws, jurisdiction and administration shall apply to any area of the land of Israel which the Government shall designate by Order.

The following day such an order was passed which included Arab Jerusalem. On 29 June 1967, an Israeli military order dissolved the Municipal Council of Arab Jerusalem. Other measures followed, expropriating Arab lands including Waqf foundations.

Quite clearly, all those measures violate international law and the Fourth Geneva Convention of 1949. On 4 July, and again on 14 July the General Assembly passed resolutions declaring all measures taken by Israel to change the status of Jerusalem null and void. On 21 May 1968, the Security Council passed a resolution endorsing the General Assembly resolutions that the acquisition of territory by military conquest was inadmissible and declaring 'that all the legislative and administrative measures and actions taken by Israel, including the expropriation of land and properties thereon, to change the legal status of Jerusalem, as null and void and cannot change that status'. Another resolution was passed on 3 July 1969 which censured the actions of Israel and its failure to comply in the strongest terms. Another resolution was passed on 15 September 1969, following the burning of al-Aqsa Mosque. All the resolutions refer to Jerusalem as 'occupied territory'. The last resolution was passed on 22 March 1979 by the Security Council on Israeli settlements in the occupied territories, including Jerusalem.[35]

In 1947–8 the Israeli terrorists forcibly occupied virtually the whole of Palestinian Arab West Jerusalem, described by distortion as Israeli Jerusalem. They expelled the inhabitants, seized their homes, furniture, lands and belongings and rendered them refugees under every sky. If anyone should have the slightest doubt about my assertion, all he need do is read the title deeds of ownership, which have been microfilmed and preserved by the British Government and passed on to the U.N. and its Palestine Conciliation Commission. The records of what belongs to whom and where it is are at present available in the archives of the U.N. for all to see and read. 'Seventy per cent Arab' was Chief Justice Sir William Fitzgerald's verdict when he delineated the zoning of the Arab and Jewish quarters in Jerusalem in 1945.

The Jewish occupation of West Jerusalem, as shown in the armistice line of 1949, running north to south, included twice as much territory as was assigned the Jews by the Fitzgerald Commis-

sion on Jerusalem. The magnitude of the injustice inflicted upon
the Palestinians can be gauged from the following figures. In 1917
the Jews owned 1.5% of the land of Palestine; by the end of the
mandate that had increased to 5.7%, including public domains
granted to them by the Mandatory Power. As a consequence of the
Israeli military onslaught against the Palestinian people, in 1947–8
the Israeli military machine occupied 73% of the total area of
Palestine.

In the Jerusalem of 1948 the Israelis militarily seized and
usurped almost the whole of new Jerusalem; we were left with what
we used to describe, in jest, by an Arabic expression which means
'the only remaining quarter', which also means that God is the only
immortal thing. In 1967 the tiny remnant was seized, including the
Old City, comprising the most sacred Islamic and Christian Holy
Places and shrines.

Throughout history neither the Arab World nor the Islamic
World has shown any intolerance towards the people of the Judaic
faith. Indeed, no Muslim would be a true Muslim if he showed
such intolerance; it would be an aberration. Also, it was the Muslims who throughout the centuries allowed the Jews back into
Jerusalem whenever they were expelled from it.

On 15 November 1949 the Governments of Lebanon, Jordan,
Syria and Egypt pledged themselves to the following declaration, in
response to an appeal by the Palestine Conciliation Commission:

> The Governments of Egypt, the Hashemite Kingdom of Jor-
> dan, Lebanon and Syria undertake to guarantee freedom of
> access to the Holy Places, religious buildings and sites situated
> in the territory placed under their authority by the final settle-
> ment of the Palestine problem or, pending that settlement, in the
> territory at present under their control by armistice agreements
> and, pursuant to this undertaking, will guarantee rights of entry
> and of transit to ministers of religion, pilgrims or visitors, with-
> out distinction as to nationality or faith, subject only to consid-
> erations of national security, all the above in conformity with the
> *status quo* prior to 14 May 1948.

The Palestine Conciliation Commission made a similar request
of Israel. The reply of the Israeli representative contained in a

letter of 8 November 1949 to the Chairman of the Palestine Commission, was that

> Israel was of the opinion that it would in the circumstances be in
> the interests of a constructive and final settlement if the matter of
> formulation were dealt with after far-reaching consideration of
> these problems by the General Assembly.

It is manifestly clear, therefore, that in spite of persistent Israeli
allegations that, during the period of unity between the West Bank
and the East Bank of Jordan, the Israelis were denied access to the
Wailing Wall, it was Israel itself which refused to make a declaration on visits to the Holy Places in Palestine similar to that made by
the Arab Governments. The reasons are self-evident: the Israelis
were determined to prevent any Palestinian from returning to his
home and homeland or visiting his Holy Places. Their minds were
set on the occupation and annexation, at a subsequent appropriate
time, of the rest of Palestine and the remnants of Arab Jerusalem –
which they carried out in 1967.

The Israeli occupation of Palestine and the whole city of Arab
Jerusalem has in fact cut off tens of millions of Christian Arabs
throughout the Middle East and hundreds of millions in the
Islamic World from performing their prayers at their Holy Places
for 30 years in three-quarters of Palestine and for over 13 years in
Arab Jerusalem and the rest of the territories occupied since 1967.
Indeed, the Palestinian inhabitants of Jerusalem are regarded as
guests and residents in their own ancestral city. They are treated as
creatures, not as human beings, and the Israeli occupiers are im-
patiently awaiting the attrition by mortality of the old, the exodus
of the young abroad for education and gainful employment – for
hardly any exists for them in their own city – to achieve their
eventual elimination. As for the Jerusalem exiles, it is hardly an
exaggeration to state that their chances of going into outer space
are far greater than their chances of attaining the elementary and
inalienable right of repatriation to their own city.[55]

Jerusalem under Israeli Occupation

The Israeli forces occupied the Arab City of Jerusalem on 7 June
1967. Thereupon they immediately proceeded to judaize the Holy
City. They embarked on the execution of their plan by confiscating
Arab lands and property, obliterating Arab and Muslim civiliza-

tion, liquidating Arab economy and the inclusion thereof in the Israeli economy. They proceeded to alter the unique characteristics of the buildings which Jerusalem had enjoyed throughout long centuries. They launched a harsh and stern campaign of terrorism against the Arab inhabitants to force them to evacuate the city, with a view to filling the vacuum so created by Jewish immigrants.

The Israeli authorities further initiated a programme of diggings and evacuations under the historical Arab and Muslim buildings, a process that resulted in the damage and cracking of hundreds thereof. Not satisfied with these machinations, the Israeli forces demolished hundreds of historical Arab and Muslim buildings. To support their actions, the Israelis put forward several allegations and unsound arguments. They pretended that such demolitions were necessitated by the need to widen and enlarge the open space near the Wailing Wall. Another of their pretences was the allegation that those buildings were in danger of falling down. The fact is, however, that those buildings would never have been in such a condition, had it not been for the excavations and diggings carried out by the forces of occupation.

By 11 June 1967 the authorities of occupation had already demolished the following:

(1) 125 houses in Al-Magharibah quarter, adjacent to Al-Aqsa Mosque. Those houses were inhabited by 650 Arabs.

(2) Two mosques: Al-Buraq as-Shareef Mosque and another mosque nearby.

(3) A factory of plastics near the Armenian quarter within the walls of Jerusalem. 200 Arab labourers were employed in the said factory.

(4) 200 houses and stores outside the city walls.

Those acts of demolition have led to the dispersal of about 1,000 of the Arab inhabitants of Jerusalem. Meantime, the authorities of occupation had already caused the dispersal of thousands of the Arab inhabitants, immediately on the heels of the occupation of Jerusalem.

The number of families so ejected from their houses was 300. The plan of confiscating Arab lands and the appropriation thereof is still being carried out. It will continue functioning until the last piece of Arab land in the City of Jerusalem is confiscated.

In an effort to give a legal aspect to the programme to judaize the city of Jerusalem, the authorities of occupation drew up a scheme for the 'Reorganization of the Holy City, within and outside the walls'. This scheme is being carried out step by step. The Israeli authorities have surrounded Jerusalem on all its sides by fortresses and citadels composed of large and high buildings, with a view to cutting off Jerusalem entirely from all Arab sectors in the West Bank.

On 27 June 1967, the authorities of occupation adopted a resolution whereby the Government of Israel was authorized to apply the 'Israeli law' in any land area which it deemed necessary to annex to Israel. The Secretary of the Government of Israel proclaimed a decree providing that 'the area of the land of Israel, as shown in the supplement appended to the decree, is subject to the law of Israel, its jurisdiction and administration'. The said supplement included the 'area of the organization of Jerusalem', namely the municipality of Jerusalem. This area was inhabited, prior to the Israeli occupation, by around 90,000 Arabs. They have come, according to this decree, and without their consent, directly under Israeli sovereignty. What was still worse, the Israeli army dissolved the legally elected Municipal Council of the Arab City of Jerusalem.

On 30 June 1967, the military authorities abolished the Jordanian laws and regulations, replaced them by Israeli laws and regulations, and set up an Israeli military body which subjected all the Arab inhabitants to its oppression and harshness.

On 4 July 1967, the Jordanian Government appealed to the U.N. against the measures and acts undertaken by the Israeli authorities. After their consideration of the Jordanian complaint, the U.N. adopted resolution 2254 on 14 July 1967, in which they: considered all the Israeli measures and acts to be void and illegal; called for the abolition of those measures and acts; and demanded of Israel to refrain and desist from taking any such measure as would lead to a change in the status of the city of Jerusalem.

Nevertheless, Israel refused to abide by the U.N. resolution, and persevered in its measures. In the meantime, Arab accusations continued to appear before the U.N. and U.N.E.S.C.O. Both bodies adopted several resolutions which strongly blamed the Israeli authorities, and called upon them to refrain from their measures and abolish them.

Yet the Israeli authorities of occupaton continued the implementation of their programme to judaize the City of Jerusalem, in the following manner:

(1) **The judaization of the Arab economy:** the authorities of occupation cut off and separated the city from the rest of the West Bank. Establishing customs offices around the city, they closed down the existing Arab banks, namely the Arab Bank, the Cairo Bank, the Jordan Bank, the Real Estate Bank, the National Bank and Intra Bank, and seized their finances. They replaced Jordanian currency by Israeli currency, the value of which has fallen in an unprecedented manner, to the detriment of the Arab inhabitants who were forced to deal with Israeli currency. The Israeli authorities subjected the Arabs to the Israeli system of taxation, including the supplementary tax and the defence tax which is collected from the Arabs for the benefit of the Israeli army which occupies their land. The application of those measures resulted in paralysis of the Arab economy and a continuous Arab migration from the city of Jerusalem to the East Bank of the River Jordan.

(2) On 25 July 1967, the authorities of occupation conducted a census in Jerusalem. The said authorities considered all Arab citizens of Jerusalem who were absent from the city (for reasons of work, education, visits, or refugees as a result of the war), as *absentees* and deprived them of their rights to return to their city. After the completion of both measures, namely the annexation of Jerusalem and the census, the Israeli authorities of occupation hastened to enforce the 'Absentee Property Law' on the Jerusalem Arabs and proceeded to register both the immovable and movable properties belonging to those Arabs so considered as absentees. Consequently, the authorities of occupation laid their hands on large areas of what remained of Arab land and property. Those were either transformed into Jewish property or placed at the disposal of the occupation authorities, exactly as was the fate of the properties of the Arabs who had been expelled, or were outside the country, in the Palestinian sectors occupied in 1948.

(3) **Confiscation and plunder of the property of Arabs residing in Jerusalem:** not satisfied with the Arab property and lands which they had seized through the application of the 'Absentee Property Law', the Israelis confiscated other large areas of Arab lands and a number of Arab buildings on the grounds that they were necessary for public services and for forests and roads. During the period 1968–76, the authorities of occupation committed the following acts of confiscation and plunder:

(a) in 1968, 4,000 dunums of land outside the city walls. Within the city walls: 595 Arab buildings, composed of 1,048 residential flats, 437 stores and commercial centres and 2 Muslim religious sites. They demolished and confiscated two mosques. These buildings and stores are in the southern part of Bab-Al-Silsilah (known as Al-Magharibah Quarter); Sharaf Quarter; Sook Al-Bashorah and Sook Al-Husor.

(b) in 1969 and 1970, 12,000 dunums. A portion of this land falls within the area of Jerusalem. The other, greater portion was confiscated from 10 Arab villages surrounding the city of Jerusalem, namely the villages of Ar-Ram, Lalandiah and Beit Hanina to the north; Nabi Samuel and Beit Iksa to the west; Beit Safafa, Sharaft and Sour Baher to the south. The Israeli authorities rased to the ground all Arab houses that were therein and drove out their inhabitants.

(c) in 1971 and 1972, 5,000 dunums of the land of the villages of Anata and El-Azariyeh, to the east of Jerusalem; they built on those confiscated lands Jewish residential quarters.

(d) in 1973, 1974 and 1975, 70,000 dunums of the lands of 'Al-Khan Al-Ahmar' – between Jerusalem and the city of Jericho; they built an industrial town, which is being enlarged at the cost of Arab lands. They further confiscated 1,630 dunums of the Nebi Samuel lands and commenced the building of residential quarters thereon.

With a view to joining occupied Arab Jerusalem with the Israeli sector occupied in 1948, the Israeli authorities proclaimed the 'Plan of Greater Jerusalem'. This plan proposes the widening and enlarging of the present boundaries of the city of Jerusalem, to include in the north the cities of Ramallah and Beereh and the adjacent Arab villages; in the south the cities of Bethlehem, Beit Jala and Beit Sahur with the adjacent villages; in the east the villages of Abu Dis, Al-Azariah, Tor, Anata Ram. By means of this plan the authorities of occupation acquire one-third of the occupied West Bank.

(4) **Demolition and fracture of Arab property within the city walls, resulting from Israeli excavation:** Pretending to dig for antiquities, the Israeli authorities of occupation carried out various excavations within the city walls, and in particular under the buildings adjoining the southern and western walls of Al-Haram as-Shareef. This led to the collapse of the property and thereafter to its demolition. This Waqf property (buildings) was used for residential, religious and cultural purposes. The demolition of those buildings led to the expulsion of a large number of the

Arab inhabitants, rendering them homeless. The aforementioned excavations caused damage to Al-Zawiyah Al-Fakrieh and 14 buildings adjoining it. The excavations also resulted in damaging and fracturing another Zawiyah (Ribat Al-Kurd) and an old Muslim school (Al-Jawhariyah).

The excavations were extended in width and depth, until they reached under the southern wall of Al-Haram as-Shareef; the lower courts of Al-Masjid Al-Aqsa; Masjid Omar, and the south-eastern halls of Al-Qasa. The said excavations now threaten with damage and collapse the mosque (Al-Aqsa) which is holy to all Muslims.

U.N.E.S.C.O has continuously censured the authorities of occupation for those excavations and demanded an immediate cessation. Nevertheless, the Israeli authorities persevere adamantly to ignore the censure of U.N.E.S.C.O. Israel still continues its excavation.

(5) **Evacuation of the Arab inhabitants from lands and property, confiscated by force, and the establishment of Jewish quarters thereon:** on 25 June 1974, the authorities of occupation announced a programme for the evacuation of 18,000 Arab inhabitants residing within the city walls of Arab Jerusalem, particularly those residing near Al-Haram as-Shareef.

The Israeli newspaper *Davar* reported in its issue of 25 June 1974 the details of the programme:

(a) a local and worldwide campaign of propaganda to spread the claim that the health standard at the Arab property within the city walls is below health and sanitary requirements and that therefore those buildings ought to be pulled down.

(b) warnings addressed to the inhabitants of those quarters to evacuate their homes, stores and workshops.

(c) the building of 750 residential flats on confiscated Arab lands east of Jerusalem, to be given to some of the families after their ejection from the old city.

Simultaneously with the continuation of this calamity, the authorities of occupation proceeded to build purely Jewish quarters on Arab lands confiscated in various parts of the West Bank. These quarters include two industrial, one military and one university, suburbs. It must be mentioned, with special emphasis, that a Jewish residential sector was built, within the city walls, on the debris of four Arab quarters. The sector is to be inhabited by 5,000 Israelis, in lieu of the 6,000 Arabs who had lived there.

(6) **Israeli acts of aggression on Muslim and Christian Holy Places in the city of Jerusalem:** these acts of aggression started with the burning of the holy mosque Al-Aqsa on 21 August 1969. The authorities of occupation had already paved the way, preliminary to the occupation of this holy sanctuary, by adopting a series of measures and instigations.

(a) the confiscation, appropriation, demolition and mining of the Waqf buildings adjoining the Al-Aqsa Mosque, to the west and south.

(b) the occupation of Bab Al-Magharibah, one of the main gates of Al-Haram as-Shareef, and the setting up therein of an Israeli military post.

(c) the conducting of demonstrations and the holding of Jewish prayers within the 'Haram' area, by members of the Israeli army, extremist Israeli organizations and fanatical religious bodies.

(d) the deepening of excavations around Al-Haram as-Shareef.

On 29 January 1976, the Israeli judiciary intervened to join other Israeli bodies in their efforts and activities of judaize the city of Jerusalem and molest and violate the religious sanctity of its holy sites by vindicating a group of young Jewish men who held prayers and caused agitation in the area of Al-Aqsa Mosque.

The Israeli acts of aggression on the Christian religious places had many aims, the most significant of which are the following:

(a) to molest and desecrate the Christian sanctuaries.

(b) to bring continuous pressure to bear on the leaders of the big Christian communities, with a view to forcing them to relinquish large areas of their land and property in Jerusalem, either by selling them or by leasing them for long periods.

(c) to terrorize the Christian religious leaders.

The Church of the Holy Sepulchre was subjected to several acts of aggression and robbery. In the last days of 1967, several Israelis stole the crown of the Virgin Mary. On 24 March 1970, the Israelis damaged the candle stands and destroyed the oil lamps hanging over the Holy Sepulchre. On 12 April 1973, three Israelis endeavoured to steal the diamond crown of the Virgin Mary, near the Cross of Golgotha in the Church of the Holy Sepulchre. They attacked a Franciscan monk, who was beaten severely. On 11 February 1974, four Christian centres in Jerusalem were burnt.

In the field of confiscating the lands of the Christian Arabs, the authorities of occupation were able to lay their hands on the following properties:

(a) the lands of the quarters of Al-Musallabeh, Katamon and Karm Arruhvan. These lands, composing large areas of the city of Jerusalem, were the property of the Greek Orthodox Patriarchate.

(b) the Schneller School with large areas of land adjoining it. The directors of the said school were forced, under duress and threats, to sell the school and the lands. The Schneller School was founded in the middle of the nineteenth century as an industrial orphanage.

(c) the land and buildings of the Russian (White) Church, in the middle of Jerusalem. The land area is wide and contains several large buildings.

(d) the 'Fast' Hotel building in the centre of Jerusalem. It was owned by the Armenian Patriarchate.

Many Christian religious leaders were subjected to acts of aggression and were beaten at the hands of the Israelis. The following are outstanding cases:

(a) on 6 February 1973, Bishop Vasilios (the second responsible leader in the Orthodox Patriarchate of Jerusalem) was beaten severely.

(b) on Christmas Day, 25 December 1970, the monks of the Coptic Convent were beaten.

(c) the arrest and detention of the Arab bishop Elaryon Kabbushi who was later sentenced, after appearing before a court – which was a mockery – to imprisonment for 12 years.

(d) the Christians in Jerusalem were subjected to oppression and continued pressure. Thousands of those Christians of Jerusalem were forced to leave the city. The following figures bear evidence to this fact:

Community	Number before the occupation 1967	Present number [1977]
Greek Orthodox	5,000	4,000
Catholic	7,000	4,000
Armenian	3,000	2,000
Other Christian communities	3,300	2,360
Total	18,300	12,360

Jewish quarters which encircle the Arab City of Jerusalem[11]

Name	Date built	Place	Class	Economic aspect and population	Original owner and area
(1) Atarot-Kalandiah		North of Jerusalem near Kalandiah Airport	Industrial	Factories	Lands appropriated by purchase and confiscation
(2) Nevi-Yacov	1973	North of Jerusalem near Shufat	Residential		Jewish settlement before 1948. Nevi-Yacov lands
(3) Ramot	1973	North-west of Jerusalem near Nebi Samuel	Residential plan for establishing 1,000 flats	8,000 people in August 1976 1,000 families in 1976	Lands appropriated by purchase and confiscation in Nebi Samuel
(4) Anatot (Anata)	Ministerial Decree in November 1974	North-east of Jerusalem	Industrial	Garages and workshops used by Arabs	3,000 dunums of Anata lands confiscated in 1972
(5) Ramat Eshkol	1968	North of Jerusalem	Residential		Previously disarmed area. By confiscation
(6) The French Mound	1969	North of Jerusalem neighbouring Mount Scopus	Residential		Confiscated lands (1968-69) 3,500 dunums confiscated for the purpose of establishing Ramat Eshkol and the French Mound: one-third owned by Arabs, one-third by Jews and one-third by the Government of Jordan. In August 1970, a further 11,680 dunums were confiscated to build suburbs north and south of Jerusalem
(7) Gheelo	1973	South of Jerusalem between Beit Safafa and Beit Jala	Residential plan for building 1,500 flats		
(8) Talpioth East	1973	East of Jerusalem south of Jabal Mukabber	Residential plan for building 3,000 flats		The village of Eastern Talpioth
(9) The Jewish Quarter in the Old City	1967	Old City of Jerusalem	Residential religious school, 200 families in April 1976		Muslim Waqf. Muslim family Waqf. Lands owned by Arabs and Jews. In June 1967, 180 houses were demolished. In April 1968, 600 houses were confiscated. In 1971, 2,000 Arabs were expelled from this quarter
(10) Baal Hetud	Under registration 1975	Tel Al-Asour			
(11) Ofra	East of Ramallah		Labour encampment for Gush Emunim		

The emigration of the Christian Arabs from Jerusalem is still continuous and the same is also true of the emigration of the Muslim inhabitants.

(7) **The judaization of Arab education:** soon after the Israeli occupation of the city of Jerusalem, the Israeli authorities laid their hands on all government schools and educational organizations. They subjected those institutions to the same Israeli curriculum which had been forced on Arabs since 1948. In their programmes of education, the Israelis have purposely left out all subjects which the Arab really needs for his national and religious education. The theory underlying this step is the desire of the Israelis to prevent the Arabs from cementing their attachment to their lands and homes and to estrange them from their basic culture and historical values. In this manner the Arab people will lose their original personality and entity, preliminary to bringing about their amalgamation in the Jewish personality and the State of Israel.

By virtue of the above-mentioned measures, about 20,000 Arab students in the city of Jerusalem are obliged to study the Israeli curriculum and Hebrew history. The Israeli educational programmes are rich with Israeli slogans such as the 'promised land' and 'the liberation of Palestine from the Arabs'. They lack any references to the history, culture and religion of the Arabs. The Israeli educational programmes aim to make the Arab students believe that 'Palestine' is a Jewish country since ancient times, in spite of the historical facts that prove beyond any doubt that 'Palestine' is Arab. Furthermore, the Israeli educational programmes prepare the Arabs psychologically to accept the Israeli expansionist schemes to undermine Arab prestige, to shake Arab self-confidence, to exaggerate Israeli progress in civilization and minimize Arab progress and advancement.

(8) **The judaization of the official Islamic judiciary:** on the heels of the Israeli occupation of Jerusalem on 7 June 1967, the Israeli authorities of occupation closed down all legal Arab courts. They removed the 'High Court of Appeal' from the City of Jerusalem to Ramallah. They amalgamated the courts of peace and the courts of first instance in Jerusalem with the Israeli courts. They demanded of Arab judges and employees to submit applications for work with the Israeli Law Ministry. They thus terminated the official judiciary that existed in Arab Jerusalem, and linked it entirely to the Israeli judiciary.

The Arab lawyers refused to appear before Israeli official and military courts and declared their refusal to recognize the annexation of Jerusalem to Israel, while the judges of the Muslim religious courts refused to cooperate with the Israeli authorities of occupation. In consequence of this stand, the authorities of occupation instructed all their organs and bodies to refrain from the execution of any judgement or order emanating from Muslim religious courts. The authorities ignored wholly any petitions of complaint presented to them by the Muslim Waqf department or by the Chairman of the Muslim Committee in Jerusalem. This Committee was formed after the occupation, to advance Muslim affairs in Jerusalem and the West Bank. The ignoring by the authorities of marriage certificates, the judgements and orders pertaining to divorce, inheritance, mandatory responsibility, Waqf and other matters of personal status of the inhabitants, including the registration of births resulting from a new wedlock. This conduct led to the creation of many human difficulties and problems.

(9) **The exile of Arab citizens:** having carried out the plan of mass expulsion of Arabs, and having subjected the Arab inhabitants of Jerusalem to psychological, bodily and economic terrorism, and with a view to evacuating the city of its national and religious leadership and weakening the Arab element in the city by depriving it of physicians, engineers and similar professions, the Israeli authorities of occupation exiled the president of the Higher Muslim Committee, the Mayor of Jerusalem, ex-ministers, notables and deputies, physicians, lawyers, college directors, teachers, agriculturists and journalists. The aim is to get rid of some of the Arab political and popular leaders and, in general, weaken the spirit of opposition and spread among the Arabs the fear of being exiled. By means of exile, the authorities would avoid another problem, namely that of detention and imprisonment. One other reason for the choice of exile rather than detention or imprisonment is the knowledge of the authorities that members of the families of the persons exiled will soon leave the city and join them.

The manner in which the sentence of exile is executed is inhuman and a violation of personal rights. The person earmarked for exile is surprised after midnight by a visit of the soldiers who carry him away in a military vehicle and prevent him from taking with him any personal clothes. In some cases the person so exiled is thrown into the Jordanian side of the desert, from whence he has to walk to reach the nearest Jordanian boundary post. By the time he reaches the post he may be on the verge of death.

(10) **Arab citizens in Israeli prisons:** the treatment by the Israeli authorities of Arab prisones and detainees and the atrocities to which they are subjected differ in no manner from the actions of the Nazis during their occupation of the peoples of Europe. The Israeli authorities apply harsh measures to break down the personality and pride of the Arab citizen. They subject him to atrocious acts and brainwashing.

It was established by the I.C.R.C. that the Israelis resort to narcotics and chemicals in their treatment of Arab prisoners and detainees. The application of electrical current on prisoners and compressing their organs are an ordinary daily machination in Israeli camps of detention. Over the last decade, 35,000 Arabs were sentenced or detained in Israeli prisons.

Besides individual acts of detention, the authorities pass mass sentences on an entire village or city. They prevent the delivery of food to such a village or city, cut off the electric current from it, and subject it to curfew orders. The Commission on Human Rights, an organ of the U.N., has censured these barbaric acts and called upon Israel to desist and refrain from their practice. The Commission has appointed a Committee to visit the Israeli prisons, to investigate the hundreds of complaints which have been received by the Commission on Human Rights and I.C.R.C. But Israel has refused to receive the Committee and has forbidden its entry into the occupied territories, on the grounds that the matter violates Israeli sovereignty.

Conclusion: The Israeli authorities of occupation were unable to achieve the minimum peaceful co-existence between the Arabs and the Israeli occupiers. Most of the Israeli newspapers and many responsible Israelis have announced their recognition of this fact. As a result of the Arab determination to refuse the Israeli occupation, the city of Jerusalem has been transormed into what is equivalent to a prison for the Arab inhabitants. They are being ceaselessly subjected to the plan of economic, political and social strangulation, in addition to mass and individual acts of detention perpetrated day and night by Israelis.

The confiscation of the lands around Jerusalem in the pretence that they are needed for 'public welfare', the transformation of the remainder of Waqf property into special zones and centres of antiquities, on the assumption of the organization of Jerusalem; the expulsion of thousands of Arab residents from the Old City and their replacement by 5,000 Jews; the endeavour of the Israelis to defend their measures on the ground of the congestion of the population on the one hand, and the alleged rights of Israel on the other hand, are all facts that have carried the case of Jerusalem to the conscience of the world.

On 29 January 1979, the Israeli Parliament's governing coalition tabled a draft law which would make Jerusalem the seat of foreign diplomatic missions. According to this law Israel will request all States with diplomatic missions in Israel to transfer their offices to Jerusalem within a certain period of time; full diplomatic immunity will be given to foreign embassies in Jerusalem only, while a minimum of diplomatic immunity will be given to embassies in Tel Aviv. Israeli ministries were instructed to deal with foreign ambassadors in Jerusalem. In September 1978, Menachem Begin decided to transfer his office and the offices of the Minister of Foreign Affairs from Tel Aviv to Jabal Al-Mukhaber in Arab Jerusalem.

In its issue of 26 March 1969 the Israeli newspaper *Ma'ariv* uncovered details of the Israeli 'Plan for Greater Jerusalem' as the capital of Israel. *Ma'ariv* pointed out that the plan was begun in June 1967, providing for increasing the population of the city eventually to 900,000, of whom the overwhelming majority would be Jews. The plan is described as:

(1) The annexation of 400–500 square kilometres of Arab land surrounding Jerusalem, from Ramallah to Bethlehem.

(2) The evacuation of no less than 130,000 Arabs from that area by any means.

(3) The division of the West Bank (it is a fact that the larger portion of this plan is being implemented in lands of Beit Jala, Anata, Jabal Tawil in El-Bireh and land from Beit Sahour).

(4) Erasing the Arab and Islamic tradition and character. Digging operations by the Israeli authorities are still going on under the western and southern wall of the Aqsa Mosque and the Buraq Wall. These diggings have reached the point where they could cause large parts of the Mosque and other historic and religious sites to cave in in ruins. This includes 300 homes, housing about 3,000 Arab citizens.

(5) The burning of the al-Aqsa Mosque on 21 August 1969.

(6) The usurpation of the Palestine Museum in Jerusalem, claimed as the property of the Israeli Government.

(7) Replacing Arab and Islamic names of streets and other historic Arab sites by Hebrew/Jewish names.

(8) The demolition of Mamilla Cemetery, the 1,000-year-old Islamic cemetery, in occupied Jerusalem since 1948, transforming it into an Israeli park.

(9) The expropriation of vast areas of Christian and Islamic land and property.

(10) The application of Israeli tax and customs laws to Arab industrial products in the city of Jerusalem, with preferential treatment to Israeli products.

(11) The application of Israeli commercial laws to Arab commercial activities, to burden Arab businessmen with high taxation.

(12) In an attempt to force bankruptcy and liquidation in the Arab Electric Company, the Israeli authorities are forcing the company to supply Israeli settlements around Jerusalem with power, without forcing these settlements to pay for it.[32]

After the occupation of the Old City, Israel embarked upon a programme to enlarge the three-metre-wide area between Al Buraq–As Sharif, or Wailing Wall, and the adjacent Moroccan and Bab-Al-Silsila quarters. Both quarters, and many others of course, were Islamic Waqf religious endowments. They consisted of hundreds of ancient and picturesque Arab homes and buildings of great artistic, historical and religious value. Their age alone entitled them to deference. They were all bulldozed to the ground. A huge assembly square opposite the Wailing Wall now covers the area where those historic buildings once stood. It is at present being used for tourists and buses, and overlooking the whole panorama are newly built villas for the habitation of Israeli ministers, military governors and other usurpers.

The Israelis occupied and confiscated most of the city of Jerusalem in 1948. The premises of the Knesset and the Hebrew University were builtlt after 1948 on Arab lands belonging to the beautiful village of Ein Karem. But apart from these and a few other instances, very little indeed was done in the field of construction in those areas over the past 30 years, not even essential maintenance and repairs. When the remaining part of Arab Jerusalem in the east, north and south was occupied in June 1967, a spurt of construction suddenly began on an unparalleled scale, not in the western section, but in the eastern; not over Jewish lands or Arab lands already confiscated since 1947–8, but over additional lands, likewise confiscated, in the east, south, north and west of an expanded Jerusalem.

It is in full awareness of this horror that the Heads of State and Government and the Ministers for Foreign Affairs of the European Council representing the European Community have joined in the near-unanimous belief of mankind, in advocating the imperative need to achieve a comprehensive and just settlement which high-lights the legitimate national rights of the Palestinian people, including, of course, self-determination, the participation of the P.L.O. as the Palestinian people's representative, an end to ter-ritorial military occupation and the illegality of settlements, and security for all. The nine Common Market countries have also recognized the special importance of the role played by the ques-tion of Jerusalem for all the parties concerned. According to the text of the Venice Declaration, the E.E.C.

stress that they will not accept any unilateral initiative designed to change the status of Jerusalem and that any agreement on the city's status should guarantee freedom of access to the Holy Places.

Even though Jordan has no illusion that the Declaration by the European Community will end occupation and redeem the Palesti-nian people's inalienable rights overnight, and while we recognize that the European Declaration is not wholly adequate as it stands and is somewhat blurred in some of its provisions, it is a vital and deeply valued tributary to a confluence which is emerging to achieve a just and comprehensive peace.

The annexation of Jerusalem and the measures which have been taken to change the status and character of the Holy City are blatantly contrary to international law, the Hague Convention of 1907, the Fourth Geneva Convention of 1949, the Universal Decla-ration of Human Rights and other relevant conventions. They are audaciously in violation of the provisions of the Charter of the U.N. which categorically prohibits the acquisition of territory by military conquest. They arrogantly defy General Assembly resolutions 2253 of 4 July 1967 and 2254 of 14 July 1967, and Security Council resolutions 252 (1968), 267 (1969), 271 (1969), 298 (1971) and, the latest one, resolution 465 (1980) of 1 March 1980.

The Islamic Conference of Foreign Ministers, meeting at its eleventh session held in Islamabad, 17–21 May 1980, viewed with the gravest alarm the all but complete devouring of Al Quds Al-Sharif (Jerusalem). The Israelis, having snuffed out the life and legacy of Jerusalem, are seemingly determined to destroy even its 1,400-year-old holiest places, the Aqsa Mosque sanctuary and the Dome of the Rock.

On 21 August 1969 a supposedly deranged man, allegedly Australian, partially succeeded in an arson attempt against the Aqsa Mosque. A month and a half ago, in the words of former Defence Minister Ezer Weizman, a horrible crime was about to be committed when two Israeli soldiers and their accomplices were apprehended with a stockpile of 264 lb. of explosives, scores of bombs, fuses and wiring. It was subsequently disclosed that the plan of the not-so-deranged but fanatical soldiers had been to blow up the venerated Aqsa Mosque and the unmatchable Dome of the Rock, so close to the hearts of almost 900 million Muslims – their first Qibla in Islam and their third holiest sanctuary. It is the spot from which the prophet Muhammad made his nocturnal journey to the heavens to witness God's infinite creation.

The plan was to have been executed on a Friday, when normally at least 100,000 civilian worshippers assemble for prayer within the two mosques and outside them, throughout the open spaces of the holy sanctuary. Thousands, of course, would have been killed, wounded and maimed. Civilization and culture would have lost one of its most ancient and priceless treasures.

For Christians and Muslims Jerusalem, with its Holy Places, is as vital as their very heart-beat, linked to their spiritual experiences and beliefs, their memories, traditions and existence over 2,000 years of profound spiritual history. If the Israelis think that Jerusalem is uniquely the spiritual centre of Judaism and of no other faith, they are disastrously and myopically wrong. The Israelis can talk in the most passionate terms about their own feelings – that is their prerogative. But they have neither the right nor the ability to gauge the infinite and undying intensity of the innermost feelings of reverence which the other two great religions hold towards Jerusalem in its spiritual and historical significance. Without the Palestinian Arab Jerusalemites, Muslim and Christian alike, there would be no Islam or Christianity in Jerusalem. The existence of the Palestinian Arabs is inextricably intertwined with the concrete embodiment of the two great religions in Jerusalem. The Palestinian Arabs are the sentinels who daily fill the churches and mosques; without them those hallowed places would become empty museums for tourists and occasional pilgrims.

Since Israel has already started the legislative process of formalizing their *de facto* annexation in basic law through the Knesset, the Foreign Ministers of the 40 Islamic States have decided, among other measures, to request the Security Council to convene in order to examine the dangers of the Israeli decision, to declare the annulment of that decision if carried through, and to impose the sanctions as stipulated in the Charter against any recalcitrant Member whose actions pose a grave threat to peace and security in the world.

Zionist intransigence has set the world on a collision course. Let us all act in concert to avoid a global catastrophe. The foremost prerequisite is the prompt Israeli withdrawal from all the occupied territories, foremost among which is Holy Jerusalem. That could be the springboard to the formulation of a just and lasting peace in the Middle East, which is the aspiration of all mankind.[55]

The latest seizure by the Israeli occupation authorities of 4,000 dunums (four million square metres) of land, to the north of occupied Arab Jerusalem, in Palestinian Arab residential areas located between Karm Louisse (the French Hill) and Qalandia Jerusalem airport, is located east of the occupied Jerusalem-Ramallah road. Radio Israel has announced that the seizure was a prelude to the construction of 12,000 new Israeli dwellings and four factories, astride a new road to link two earlier, illegally established quarters, and further to tighten the ring of strangulation on what has remained of Arab Jerusalem and its environs, extending from Bethlehem to Ramallah.[50]

To make doubly certain – as though millennia of glorious Palestinian existence can be erased by a decree – on 30 July 1980 the Knesset passed a 'basic law' which states that Jerusalem, complete and united, is the eternal capital of Israel; that Jerusalem is the seat of the President of the State, the Knesset, the Government and the Supreme Court. The Security Council responded forcefully and promptly to this most reckless challenge to international law and to the Fourth Geneva Convention of 1949 by deciding unanimously that all these measures are null and void and should be rescinded. The dozen or so Member States which had embassies in occupied West Jerusalem reacted equally vehemently by withdrawing their embassies from Jerusalem.[59]

If there is to be a peaceful solution, the question that should haunt us all is: where are the Palestinian returnees to settle. . . even the returnees or displaced persons from the West Bank and Gaza presently in Jordan who number a quarter of a million souls? What is most striking and meaningful is that during the decade of occupation, the Israelis did very little indeed to settle the considerable empty spaces in the four-fifths of Palestine which they already had in 1948. Worse still, many built-up areas are vacant and unoccupied because there are not enough people to import for settlement there, while the Palestinian refugees continue to languish in the squalor of encampments. It is no exaggeration that if a Palestinian were to visit his ancestral homeland in Palestine, he would find less difficulty recognizing Jaffa or Acre as he was forced to leave it in 1947–8 than he would Jerusalem and the heartland of the West Bank which was occupied in 1967.[13]

10
Desecrations at Hebron and Elsewhere

Information received from the Government of Jordan
Soon after the war of June 1967, the Jewish settlers directed their attention to the town of Al-Khalil (Hebron). Early in 1968, Rabbi Moshe Levinger and a group of his partisans trekked to the western outskirts of Al-Khalil where they decided to settle forcibly, even without a decision by the Israeli Government. Within a few days these settlers were effectively able to lay the foundation-stone for the settlement which is today known as Kiryat Arba'. It is so planned as to compete as a town with Al-Khalil and, later on, be called 'Al-Khalil–Alet' following the example of 'Nazareth–Alet'.

Although initially the establishment of this settlement was rather modest and met with a sort of resigned official disapproval and silence, it soon began to expand and extend and considerable budgets were provided with a view to enlarging it, increasing the number of its settlers and supplying it with such vital facilities as water, electricity, telephones, schools and synagogues.

The first step in a plan aimed at the gradual seizure of all of Al-Khalil, as well as all the surrounding Arab areas, was the establishment and consolidation of Kiryat Arba'. As actual practice has shown, the Jewish settlers wanted to make Kiryat Arba' a point of departure for their subsequent attacks against Al-Khalil. While the settlement of Kiryat Arba' was the beginning of a Jewish move to settle in the area of Al-Khalil and its suburbs, other subsequent events were aimed at the town of Al-Khalil itself. Those events took place appropximately three years after the consolidation of the settlement of Kiryat Arba'. This time, however, it was Rabbi Meir Kahane, leader of the Jewish Defence League, who assumed the leadership of the settlement campaign, which took on a religious character.

On 27 August 1972, Kahane succeeded in entering Al-Khalil with 100 of his followers. They hypocritically prayed near the holy Al-Ibrahimi Mosque. During the prayers, Kahane delivered a speech in which he announced his determination to settle the question of repatriating those whom he called 'displaced Jews' from Al-Khalil. At the time some people thought that the matter could be settled if the Jews were allowed to pray in or visit the holy Al-Ibrahimi Mosque. Meanwhile, the occupation authorities announced their disapproval of the provocations perpetrated by Meir Kahane's group.

That was the beginning of the Jewish move, which assumed a religious character, to settle in the heart of Al-Khalil. Thereafter, events occurred in the following sequence:

(1) The occupation authorities allowed the Jews to visit Al-Ibrahimi Mosque and pray there in a non-demonstrative manner and at times when Muslim prayers were not being said. This took place late in June 1972.

(2) The occupation authorities took the decision permitting Jews to pray at times when Muslim prayers were being said at Al-Ibrahimi Mosque, provided that Muslims praying were not disturbed. This step came in response to the request made both by the Jews praying at Al-Ibrahimi Mosque and the so-called Popular Committee of Kiryat Arba's Jewish citizens, early in July 1972 (newspaper *Haaretz*, 7 September 1972). Rabbi Kahane then received the approval of Al-Khalil's Military Governor allowing him and his followers to pray collectively at Al-Ibrahimi Mosque on the evening of the Day of Atonement, 17 September 1972, and at 10 a.m. the following day.

(3) On 11 November 1972, Al-Khalil's Israeli Military Governor decided to increase the hours of prayer allocated to Jews at Al-Ibrahimi Mosque. This decision was carried out as from 1.30 p.m. Friday. A number of chairs for Jews to sit on during prayers and two closets — one of which was placed in the Jacobean Corner — were introduced into the Mosque. This decision was followed by continuous actions by the Jewish settlers through which they man-

aged to seize large sections of Al-Ibrahimi Mosque, including the area which was provided with a ceiling, the Jacobean Corner, the Al-Ibrahimi Mausoleum and the Machpela Cave, in spite of the outcries, condemnation and protests of religious and popular bodies on the West Bank.

(4) In the meantime, on 3 October 1972, the Israeli newspaper *Davar* published an article by one of its editors, Danny Rubinstein, in which he clearly disclosed Zionist intentions regarding not only Al-Ibrahimi Mosque but the whole of Al-Khalil as well. The article contained the following excerpt:

> The Jewish settlers have now attained their aim. Some of them feel satisfied because their struggle is taking the form of asking for an additional half-hour of prayer, or praying inside the Mosque in a loud voice. For this purpose they can mobilize a far larger part of Israeli public opinion than the support which they could obtain if they demanded the annexation of the town of Hebron to the State of Israel.
>
> However, the settlers will not cease to arouse Israeli public opinion until the Jewish people have obtained full rights to the Mosque and until the town of Hebron has become subject to Israeli sovereignty and jurisdiction like any other Israeli town.

(5) Since the Israeli authorities divided Al-Ibrahimi Mosque in August 1975 in compliance with the orders of the Israeli Minister for Defence to assign the largest part of the Mosque to become a synagogue – which part contains the bulk of the Islamic heritage – Muslims, whose forefathers had built the Mosque and said their prayers in it for many centuries, have been deprived of the right to perform their rites and exercise their religious rights freely and their access to the Mosque has been confined to just one side-door. The same authorities restricted the area where Muslim prayers can be said to a narrow space of the Mosque facing the prayer niche which can accommodate two rows of worshippers. In addition, Israeli visitors have annoyed Muslims while the latter were praying. In July 1976, some Israeli fanatics deliberately defied the feelings of Muslims when they entered Al-Ibrahimi Mosque and tore up Allah's Scriptures – the Holy Quran – inside the Mosque, thus provoking the Muslims, who rose up against this desecration, staging demonstrations in protest. Thereupon the Israeli authorities

imposed a curfew in the town and arrested the teacher at Al-Ibrahimi Mosque, Sheikh Hafez Mohamed Heidar el-Tabri, accusing him of having instigated the resistance (to Israeli aggression).

(6) On 8 August 1976, a group of members of the Israeli Knesset belonging to various blocs delivered a memorandum to the Israeli Minister for Defence, Shimon Peres, in which they called upon him to issue instructions to the Government military authorities on the West Bank with a view to permitting Jews to settle in three buildings inside the town of Al-Khalil, claiming that prior to 1948, those buildings had belonged to various Jewish institutions and adding that this was meant to create a Jewish presence in the town of Al-Khalil, so that Kiryat Arba' might not turn into a mere Jewish enclave inside an Arab area. On 9 August 1976 the newspaper *Masriv* mentioned the names of the Knesset members who took this initiative, that is, Yadidia Berry, Cuela Cohen, Mates Drobles, Abraham Freddege, Pessach Grupper, Mathilda Guez, Eliezer Shostak and Hilel Seidel. Those members belong to the blocs Maarakh, Liberal, Likud and the Torah Front. They met with the Rabbi of Kiryat Arba', Moshe Levinger, who informed them that the settlers of Kiryat Arba' intended to transform the three buildings into a Jewish synagogue and a religious boarding school.

On 14 and 15 August 1976, a large group of Kiryat Arba' settlers and members of Gush Emunim staged an angry demonstration in the streets of Al-Khalil, demanding settlement in the city and waving their knives and axes in a provocative way. On the following day, 16 August 1976, a group of settlers from Kiryat Arba' tried to seize the Dabawia building in Al-Khalil. Members of this group beat a number of the townspeople and insulted them. Those events have come to be a campaign of incitement in the Israeli press.

About 4,000 Jews took part in the march of 16 August. They included Rabbi Shlomo Goron, the two Ministers Yosef Borg and Zebolon Hammer and a number of the members of the Israeli Knesset. Rabbi Goron delivered a speech in front of the Jewish cemetery in the town, in which he called for the reconstruction of the cemetery in order to, as he put it, rehabilitate the Jews.

On 19 August 1976, Arab citizens of Al-Khalil were surprised to see a group of Jewish workers from among the settlers of Kiryat Arba' digging under some of the buildings at Al Nahlah site which connects the main commercial market place with the vegetable market, and carrying out demolition work in these buildings. Fear-ing that clashes might take place, the Israeli security forces arrested them but released them the following day, when they returned to the town and stormed one of its buildings, where they said a prayer. One of them went up to the roof where he fixed a sign carrying the name of a Jewish synagogue.

The same opeation was repeated on 22 August 1976 when a group estimated to consist of 40 settlers forced their way into the Dabawia building, went up to the roof, danced, beat drums and shouted. Newspapers reported that the Israeli police arrested eight of them.

Provocations by Israeli settlers against the population of Al-Khalil and attempts to settle inside the town are still going on. Recently these provocations have increased, despite statements by Shimon Peres to the effect that his Government is determined to stop settlers from their continued provocations, which have developed to the degree of trying to commit aggression against Sheikh Mohamed Aly El Jaabary, ex-Mayor of Al-Khalil, in his home. Furthermore, settlers started trying to expand the settlement of Kiryat Arba' so that it encompasses most of the hills of Al-Khalil. At present, the occupation authorities prevent Arab citizens from carrying out construction work on their lands in the vicinity of Kiryat Arba'.[1]

The imprisonment of a whole city of 60,000 people – for 16 days on end, without even the judicial process of a warrant from a judge; an Israeli civilian with a machine-gun in a moving car killing, in cold blood, seven innocent Palestinian Arab bystanders, in nearby Hahlhul: we seem to have grown numb and insensitive to such atrocious behaviour because they are daily occurrences throughout the length and breadth of the West Bank and Gaza. Some of us may have seen bits and pieces of such events on the T.V. screen, thanks to a few wily and diligent correspondents who managed to circumvent the ubiquitous Israeli censor. The seizure of one of the holiest Muslim sanctuaries, Al-Haram al-Ibrahimi as-Shareef, in Hebron, and its gradual but systematic conversion into a synagogue, leaving tiny and constricted crannies to Muslim worshippers; the trampling-upon and tearing-up of the Holy Qurán, is no longer apparently a shocking and disgraceful act of vandalism which evokes spontaneous and universal condemnation, regardless of one's faith, creed or philosophy.

It is perhaps most revealing that, in the statement issued by the

Ministry of Al-Awqaaf – in charge of religious sites and charitable foundations in Jordan – the emphasis was on the disrespect shown by the trespassers on the site which is supposedly sacred to Muslims and Jews alike. The statement relates *inter alia* that in the course of their trespassing, they had indulged in immoral acts. They would resort to molesting the Muslims as they were performing their prayers, addressing derogatory, insulting and provocative remarks and shouting, at the top of their voices, to inconvenience the worshippers. This is not the way one would expect an ancient and revered sanctuary such as the Ibrahimi Mosque to be treated, by those who claim they find sustenance in its eternal spiritual message. It is not a place for picnicking or museum touring. It is very much, today as it has always been for countless centuries, a place for worship and meditation, and its sacredness should under no circumstances, including military occupation, be infringed and compromised.[2]

On 31 January 1980, an Israeli soldier was shot by an unknown assailant acting on his own in reaction to the unending and mounting provocations and assaults by the Israeli colonizers of Kiryat Arba', overlooking the city of Hebron. The soldier died of his wounds. Such incidents are a daily occurrence in most countries of the world. The police forces in such cases investigate the incident with a view to ascertaining the identity of the assailant, in accordance with the normal processes of law. Instead, the Israeli occupiers imposed a 23-hour curfew, for 11 days and nights on end, on the inhabitants of Hebron, men, women and children, subjecting them to grave hardships. The Israelis went on a rampage. Large contingents of Israeli troops subjected the inhabitants to ruthless, systematic and abusive searches, including indiscriminate break-ins into the homes of the hapless civilians, physical assaults and the destruction of furniture and other belongings. Al-Khalil was sealed off and barriers were erected across roads leading in and out of the city, thus disrupting all communications, isolating Hebron from the rest of the world and forbidding the population from visiting the East Bank and causing their perishable fruits and vegetables to rot.

The Muslim inhabitants were prohibited from performing their Friday prayers in the Holy Sanctuary of al-Haram al-Ibrahimi Mosque.

Not since the Middle Ages has a place of worship belonging to one religious affiliation been converted into a place of worship for another. The Ibrahimi Holy Sanctuary has to all intents and purposes (especially the spacious main hall of the Mosque) been converted into a synagogue, in violation of the centuries-old *status quo*.

To aggravate this provocative behaviour, they encouraged the colonizers, curfew notwithstanding, to pray illegally at this Islamic sanctuary. These colonists engaged in widespread stone-throwing at the homes of the confined inhabitants. A member of the attackers fired a machine-gun at the population. Such 'collective punishment', though not the first or the last, is reminiscent of the atrocious practices associated with the fascist occupiers of Europe during World War II of which the Jews themselves were among the foremost victims. Even more ominous is the taking-over of the Ibrahimi Holy Sanctuary which the Muslims had built well over 1,000 years ago, leaving to the Muslims small crannies and cramped spaces to perform their worship. The Israelis have already named it a synagogue.

As usual, the Israelis utilized the occasion to stretch further and fast in their policy of colonization.

On 10 February, the Israeli Council of Ministers decided to allow the Jews to settle in al-Khalil (Hebron) as, in their words, in other parts of the land of Israel. The Israeli Minister of Education urged, in addition to settling Jews in the heartland of the city, the construction of 1,000 additional housing units at Kiryat Arba', on lands confiscated recently from Tel-el-Jaabra and other lands adjacent to Kiryat Arba'.

Other Ministers demanded the resignation of Mayor Fahd el-Qawasmi and immediate settlement in the 16 houses which belonged to the Jews in the past. The Mayor retorted that he did not object to the 16 Jewish families living there, provided the over two million Palestinian home-owners of Jaffa, Haifa, Lydda, Ramleh, Asqalan and inhabitants of other towns and villages were allowed back to their homes in accordance with natural justice, international law and resolution 194 of the U.N.[48]

One of the most hallowed Muslim cemeteries, the Ma'manallah which, during the British Mandate, was shortened to Mamilla, in the western section of Jerusalem, is at least 1,000 years old. It contains the remains of men great by any standard, in all fields of achievement – saints, warriors, leaders of men and historical figures. What is its present fate? I should like one of the Americans residing in the American Consulate in Jerusalem (because that consulate is contiguous to the cemetery) to tell us what the fate of the Mamilla cemetery is. It is a public park for humans and animals to trample over, as any visitor to Jerusalem can see for himself.

As for the shrine of a great religious leader in Jaffa, which dates back several hundred years, if anyone happens to visit Jaffa and feels like having a drink in exotic surroundings, he could go there, walk down a few steps and see for himself.

The mosques of Safad and Tiberius have been converted into art galleries, and I need hardly remind you of the attempt to burn down the Al-Aqsa Mosque, which was of course attributed to a deranged Australian.

Mr Evan M. Wilson has this to say in his book, *Jerusalem, Key to Peace:*

> After the war of 1967 Christian authorities who had been unable for many years to visit certain Christian properties on Mount Zion. . . because they were. . . closed off by the Israeli military, found that some of these institutions had suffered severely [that is, on the Mount of Olives]. The tombs of the Armenian Patriarchs, in the courtyard of the Armenian Church of St Saviour, had been broken into and the bones scattered about.
>
> A famous mosaic floor had been removed from the church during or just after the war, and the church itself was in a deplorable state of disrepair. Several Christian cemeteries in the vicinity were in bad condition, with thick vegetation and opened graves. . . There is reason to believe, moreover, that this vandalism. . . is continuing. It was found in the spring of 1968, after the war, that the crosses on 83 tombs in the Catholic cemetery on Mount Zion had been shattered. It was in this area also that the tower of the Dormition Abbey was used for many years as an Israeli machine-gun nest.[5]

The Al-Aqsa Mosque sanctuary has been subjected to continuous drilling to a depth of 10–15 metres which, of course, threatens the whole structure. Also the Sayyiduna Al-Khalil Mosque sanctuary in Hebron has been virtually converted into a synagogue. These are simply examples of the desecration of Holy Places. Many other Holy Places have since been destroyed in the Old City of Jerusalem.[52]

11
The United Nations Relief and Works Agency

Back in 1957, I happened to be Undersecretary of the Ministry of Reconstruction in charge of the refugees. The newly appointed Commissioner-General and his assistant visited me to propose the establishment of a technical department to handle work programmes for the refugees. Even though many refugees felt deeply and sincerely that accepting such a project might result in their settlement outside their homeland, I managed to convince them that their repatriation was not contingent on accepting private self-sustaining projects, but on wider national and international efforts. At any rate, I asked the U.N.R.W.A. executive, how much funding do you have for this purpose, in order to gauge the size of the proposed technical division. The executive answered: $60–70 million. So we proceeded with the programme until I managed to get the Agency to spend $3 million. Then, one day, they came to me and said: Sorry, we have to stop the programme because of lack of funds. I said: What about the $60–70 million that appears for rehabilitation in every Report? Their answer was that this money was merely a pledge which did not exist in fact, and besides every dollar was needed to bolster up the diminishing working capital. . . [4]

1975–6

There are two interrelated themes which seem to overshadow, if not haunt, the otherwise exemplary Report of the Commissioner-

General. This is not so much a faulty assessment by the Commissioner-General as it is a reflection of a more fundamental failure on the part of the world community to appreciate, in full measure, its unalterable responsibility towards the tragic fate of the Palestine refugees until such time as they are enabled to go back to their homes, lands and properties. It was the U.N. which, by partitioning their country, set in motion the traumatic events which resulted in their dispersal. And it was, likewise, the U.N. failure over the past 25 years to implement its resolutions pertaining to their redemption. It is for these reasons that the guidance which the Commissioner-General seeks from the Assembly should be forthright and categorical. What the U.N. affords to the Palestine refugees is not charity, but a bare minimum assistance to survive, pending restoration of their inalienable rights in their homeland.

The twin themes which run through the Report of the Commissioner-General are: (a) because of U.N.R.W.A.'s precarious fiscal situation, the Agency may be forced to cut back considerably from its relief assistance and services for the refugees; (b) there may arise a contingency in which U.N.R.W.A. operations would almost cease to function for lack of funding.

Out of 1,668,205 registered refugees, less than one-half (49.5%) receive the relief ration of the Agency. Simple arithmethic tells us that with a relief budget of $46.6 million, after deducting administrative costs, the ration per refugee, including supplementary feeding and shelter, amounts to $4 per month, that is about $0.13 per day. It is also a fact that the basic ration does not constitute a balanced diet and is deficient in vitamins and other ingredients whose absence will have long-term adverse effects.

Furthermore, the application of the ration ceiling has resulted in the exclusion of 471,015 young children who should normally be eligible. It is therefore of utmost importance that the supplementary feeding programme be expanded, on the most up-to-date medical and scientific basis, to save a whole population of children in their most crucial formative years.

If the figures and facts I have just cited testify to anything, it is to the incredible tenacity, resilience, sacrifice, hard work and all-out dedication of the Palestinian people, to ensure survival in a merciless world.

The number of displaced refugees permitted to return to their homeland and camps is slightly less than 8,800. This reflects the degree of deference which Israel accords to General Assembly resolutions made repeatedly since 1967, and in open defiance of which they put up varying excuses to suit varying situations.

In Gaza, the situation in housing is as follows: in July–August 1971 the occupation authorities had demolished 7,729 shelters, accommodating 15,855 persons. The number of families given free accommodation is a mere 67 families. The present situation is as follows: a total of 12,544 shelter rooms affecting 4,736 refugee families were demolished between July 1967 and 30 June 1976. The shelters which the occupation authorities have constructed is around 3,070 housing units, thereby perpetuating a serious housing shortage. These housing units, incidentally, are offered for sale (not as free replacement housing) with initial financial loans against mortgage.

The education programme of U.N.R.W.A. is undoubtedly the most useful assistance rendered to the Palestine refugees. Almost 290,000 refugee children attended in the school year 1975–6, in spite of limited funds and a modest school construction programme. An additional 85,000 pupils attended private and government schools. Expenditure on education totalled $59 million in 1976, representing 46.5% of the Agency's budget, such expenditures constitute an increase of only 14% in consequence of rising costs and inflation.

There has been a continual decrease in the volume of scholarships for higher education. The dwindling number of scholarships is reflected in the following figures: in 1972 the number was 687; in 1973, 455; in 1974, 370; in 1975, 331; and in 1976, only 314 scholarships were awarded.

The U.N.R.W.A. educational programme is probably the cheapest in terms of input-output, and highest in benfit-cost ratio, that has ever been undertaken anywhere. It is incredible how nearly 300,000 pupils obtain education with a budget of only $56 million in a world of spiralling inflation.

Jordan, as host country to hundreds of thousands of refugees and one of the least endowed materially, has made direct governmental assistance to the displaced persons and refugees, for the period of 1 July 1975 to 30 June 1976, amounting to $23.5 million. But there are limits to what a small host country like Jordan can do, and a crying need for increased sharing of responsibility by the U.N. as a whole.[3]

1976–7

U.N.R.W.A. was created in 1950 to perform a temporary relief function for those Palestinians who had been forcibly ousted from their ancestral homeland, homes, properties and means of productive employment. The Agency's role, as envisaged by the U.N., was to keep body and soul together, pending their repatriation to their homeland, in accordance with resolution 194, passed by the General Assembly on 11 December 1948, which asserted the inalienable right of the Palestinian refugees to repatriation as the first choice, or compensation for those not choosing to exercise this right. The resolution is reiterated every year, but to no avail. Not a single refugee has been repatriated.[14]

This should be the fundamental framework and the core of what the General Assembly should regard as the real and final solution. It is morally and legally bound to do so, because all else is a mere palliative, while the plight of the Palestinian refugees, totalling 1.75 million human beings, is inhumanly prolonged.[28]

Compounding the original sin and tragedy of 1948 came the traumatic dispersal of yet another category of Palestinians, subsequent to June 1967, who came to be known as the displaced inhabitants, whether refugees or inhabitants of cities, towns and villages in the occupied territories. The report on the current financial situation of U.N.R.W.A. describes it:

U.N.R.W.A. has been in financial crisis since 1974 and will remain in this position until the general level of income catches up with the higher general level of budgeted expenditures, reached as a result of the rapid inflation and dollar depreciation in the years 1972–5. Inflation is not increasing as rapidly as in the past and dollar depreciation appears temporarily to have halted; but before these favourable developments took place, inflation and dollar depreciation had forced U.N.R.W.A's budgeted expenditures up to a new level, about $45 million above the current level of regular contributions.

The report adds that in the circumstances the Agency has had to rely more and more on special contributions, pledged during the year in which the income must be used.

In such unpredictable circumstances, the Agency cannot provide services to refugees in an orderly way, and at times cannot provide some services at all. During this year the Agency has had to halve its already minimal and meagre rations.

The situation has assumed such alarming proportions over the past two years, that the Agency has had to cut deep into its basic services, thus multiplying the hardships which the refugees – already the size of a nation – have been enduring for so long. It has also faced, on certain occasions, the prospects of total collapse. The crisis of the Agency has not been created by expanding services, or affording the Palestine refugees a better or higher level of living or training. Nor has it been the result of waste or inefficiency. It is simply that the worldwide phenomena of inflation and depreciation have rendered the old regular contribution out of step with the needs and realities of the later 1970s.

The Agency provides assistance to eligible refugees – although by no means to *all* eligible refugees – in three fields and in the following priorities:

(1) education and training services, at a total annual cost, including a share of common Agency costs, of $54.8 million in 1976 and an estimated $66.1 million in 1977. This includes the general education programme under which about 300,000 refugee children receive elementary and preparatory education in 595 U.N.R.W.A/U.N.E.S.C.O. schools. The education also includes vocational and teacher-training programmes under which 4,141 trainees receive training at eight U.N.R.W.A. training centres.

(2) a programme of subsidization of secondary education, under which 29,272 refugee students are educated at government secondary schools.

(3) a university scholarship programme under which 326 young refugee men and women are educated at universities in Arab countries.

It is incredible how more than 300,000 pupils obtain education, with a budget of less than $55 million, in a world of spiralling inflation. The answer is that our students and their teachers do not incur heating costs, lavishly constructed schools or even the benefit of electricity. A waterproof tent, a simple chair and bench and textbooks are all they ask for. The commitment of the Palestine refugees to education, the dedication of the teaching staff of the Agency, and the staunch cooperation of the host governments, explain the extraordinary achievements in the field of education at so bare a cost. There is also a multiplier effect in a substantially expanded higher education programme. Because of the staunch sense of family cohesion among the Palestinian refugees, the education of one son or daughter amounts to the education of all the offspring in the family. Like a chain reaction, the first educated takes it upon himself to educate the second, and the second, the third and fourth. This is the real Palestinian refugees' miracle, which very few know about or acknowledge. They don't do it for propaganda headlines, as others with far less endurance and sacrifice do. They do it because they are a resilient people who will never allow adversity to daunt them, less still to overwhelm them.

The U.N. and certain specialized agencies contribute about 4% of U.N.R.W.A's income, and non-governmental organizations about 1%. As for the remaining 95% of the Agency's budget, this must come from voluntary contributions by governments.

There are 1,706,486 registered refugees, an increase from 1976 of 38,281. Out of this total, only 821,785 are eligible for all services and full rations because of a ceiling of 800,000 imposed several years ago on the number of recipients which the Agency can afford. The great tragedy is that the hardships arising from the arbitrary ceiling presently fall almost entirely upon the newborn infants and children who number 510,706. This unfortunate category is eligible and registered for services only, but not for relief.[14]

1977–8

The number of registered refugees is presently 1,757,269. The total budget for the year [1977–8] was $139,800,000 and even this modest amount suffered an $11 million deficit. The share of the refugee is $6.50 a month, that is $0.21 a day.

A ceiling of 800,000 refugees had been placed on those eligible for assistance. The remaining 900,750, though eligible, do not receive any assistance. The irony of it is that those not receiving assistance because of the ceiling include over half a million children.

Another revealing breakdown of the 831,000 eligible and recipients of Agency assistance is as follows: basic food assistance for refugees per year is $40.33. This is equal to $3.39 per month, $0.11 per day. Of the 307,000 pupils eligible for education, a pupil's cost per month is $20.00. The cost of an eligible refugee per year for medical care is $15.00, which represents $1.25 per month.

I have mentioned the figures simply to highlight the dichotomy between the international community's verbal commitment to the cause of the Palestinian people on the one hand and its abysmal failure to match it with deeds on the other. By contrast, every Israeli man, woman and child – three million in all – receives $1,000 per annum from one country alone; and those are the same people who have deprived the Palestinians of their country and means of livelihood. They are even getting $1 billion as so-called compensation for abandoning two military airports, which they had illegally constructed over an occupied territory which they should never have occupied in the first place.

I do not blame the Commissioner-General for abandoning so many of the basic responsibilities, such as reducing the basic flour ration per month per person from 10 kg to 6.7 kg. Let me emphasize that the actual percentage of refugees receiving all services is considerably less than 17.5% of the registered refugee population. This is a far cry from the U.N. commitment to all the refugees when the Agency was created.

In the coming fiscal year, the Commissioner-General intends to follow the practice of establishing each year as early as possible a list of suspended budgeted expenditures equal to the deficit, and moving them from the non-approved to the approved category only as pledges of additonal income are received. This is an unprecedented method of drawing up and implementing a budget. In plain language, it means a gradual winding-up and dissolution of the international community's commitment to the Palestinian refugees without a corresponding resolution of their real problem.

The suspended budgeted expenditures include, of all things, a drastic reduction in preparatory education, which is so essential to enable the refugees to stand on their own two feet. Apart from the host governments, a few major contributors and insubstantial contributions by about 50–60 States, the majority of Member States are watching what is happening, unconcerned.[22]

1978–9

This annual ritual of reviewing the work of U.N.R.W.A., and hence the fate of the dispossessed people of Palestine, has been a gruesome exercise, where the temptation is great to rewrite the former year's statement, make the necessary adjustments in some facts and figures, and advance the year of the calendar.

There is, indeed, little room for innovation, less still for a fundamental structural transformation. In fact, what we have been confronting over the years or, more correctly, over the past three decades is a gradual but decidedly perceptible (if not calculated) process of shrinkage, in an onward drift towards dissolution and potential disintegration.

In plain figures, the estimates in June 1979 indicate that the Agency would be able to avoid a deficit only by not implementing – by abandoning – over $28 million of its adjusted budget of $166.3 million. This has meant that in 1979 the Agency faced the necessity of reducing substantially its education programme by closing its preparatory-cycle schools as early as 1 July 1979. Improved income had made it possible at least to postpone the school closures for a few additional months. The deficit likewise took its heavy toll of other essential obligations, including the meagre and substandard rations and other services and contractual obligations towards its 16,000 non-international Palestinian employees.

If elemental assistance to the Palestinian refugees has been sordidly bleak for 1979, the forecasts for 1980 verge on the terminal. The proposed budget for 1980 is estimated at $185.3 million, while income (with prospective reasonable assurance) is estimated at $50 million, with no assurance whatsoever of a repetition of last-minute salvage assistance which had ameliorated somewhat the 1979 deficit of close to $30 million.

There are placed before us two options, in a situation which can only be described as an impossible one. The two courses of action are as untenable as they are brutal, immoral and in flagrant violation of the General Assembly's two-fold trust towards the Palestinian people: (a) to reduce the Agency's rate of expenditure from 1 January 1980 to the level of income then foreseeable to the end of 1980, even though this means temporary or even permanent reduction of minimal basic services. It is what we deplored last year as the suspended budgeted expenditures equal to the deficit, throwing overboard basic services. This is what might be described as a prescription for death by prolonged illness, since the Agency's mandate is required to continue until 30 June 1981; (b) death by heart-stroke. This means a continuation of the reduced basic services until funds are exhausted and the Agency finds itself with no alternative but to declare its bankruptcy and consequent collapse. The Agency feels it is prudent to follow the first option.

There is nothing unique about declaring bankruptcy in the business world. Many suffer such a fate in consequence of mismanagement, bad luck or inadequacy of demand for their product. But it certainly would be unique and tragic if that should befall a U.N. Agency which had committed none of those errors. And when I talk about the Agency, I talk, of course, about the victimized Palestinian people.

There is hardly a parallel to a whole population being reduced by savage dispersal, uprooting and dispossession, for 30 years, to an enforced refugee status, precluded from earning an honourable and decent living by utilizing their lands, farms, houses and factories, and the opportunities for gainful employment which the private and public facilities of every country, such as ports, airports, railways, public domains and natural resources, afford to its people. The psychological distress of dispersal for three decades is even more lethal and colossal, though it is impossible to measure in concrete terms except by one who has been its victim. On the one hand, their hands are tied behind their backs; on the other, they are told, through failure sufficiently to support the rock-bottom needs of a human being through U.N.R.W.A., to go hungry or undernourished, to live within congested three-by-four-metre asbestos, floorless huts, where their mattress is the soil, a drenched soil in winter; where most of their schools are housed in tents with two or three shifts to accommodate the student body of several hundred thousand. And even this bare minimum has been seriously threatened by discontinuation for lack of funds and can just squeeze through up to the end of this year unless funding is made available.

The Jordanian Government, as one of the host countries, has communicated on several occasions its profound concern over the destabilizing consequences of throwing hundreds of thousands of destitute students out of school; or of further diminishing what is already a subhuman food assistance; or of abandoning the sick to wither away. It is the earnest hope of my Government that its repeated warnings will not be taken lightly for they affect directly, in one way or another, the 1,803,564 refugees registered up to 30 June 1979.

Even though there is a ceiling of 830,000 Palestinian refugees who presently receive assistance – less than half the eligible refugees, and certainly less than the refugee population which declined to register in the first place – it is this category, and particularly the close to 34% living in the indescribable squalor of the refugee camps, who stand to bear the brunt of the international community's diminishing concern as indicated by paucity of action.

The priorities in the allocation of available funds is the best under the circumstances, namely 55.5% for education, 25.7% for relief, 16.1% for health and 2.7% for other costs.

I have consistently drawn attention to the fact that the allocation of university scholarships has dwindled from over 600 to a mere 300. On 18 December 1978, the General Assembly adopted a resolution appealing to all governments and specialized agencies to contribute scholarships, in view of U.N.R.W.A.'s inability to augment this important programme, through lack of funds. Regrettably the response, in concrete terms, has been far below all reasonable expectations.

The representatives of the host governments have expressed serious and understandable apprehension that the continuing diminution of U.N.R.W.A.'s services is intended to place the entire burden of the plight of the refugees on the shoulders of the host governments, over and above their existing responsibilities. This is unacceptable on two grounds: (a) it represents the dissociation of the U.N. from its solemn obligations towards the Palestinian refugees before any step has been taken for their redemption, in accordance with the U.N. legal, moral and historical solemn obligations towards them; (b) it would place an unbearable burden upon host countries with limited means, in an issue which had been created by the U.N. itself who, therefore, should assume full responsibility for its disastrous and seemingly unending consequences.

The Advisory Commission explored various avenues for salvaging the situation. These included the utilization by U.N.R.W.A. of the revenues of the Palestinian refugees' properties and assets, which would vastly exceed the needs of U.N.R.W.A. but which presently go to the insatiable coffers of those who uprooted them, and are being handled by what is called the custodian of absentee owners, an ironical term since those so-called absentees have been forcibly prevented from returning to their country. It has also been suggested that the U.N. itself should cover, from its own budget, the deficits which have been afflicting the Agency and thwarting its solemn humanitarian task.[42]

1979–80

The Agency finds itself with no alternative but to default on the

solemn mandate entrusted to it by the General Assembly:
U.N.R.W.A. definitely plans to abandon, within the coming fiscal
year 1 July 1980–30 June 1981, some of its basic programmes,
having over the past years undergone a gradual process of shrinkage and a helpless drift towards dissolution and final disintegration.

This, I need hardly state, is being forced upon the Agency by an
act of political will, clearly designed to change the original equation, namely international responsibility and assistance pending
Palestinian redemption. A unilateral alteration of the equation
against the fundamental rights of the Palestinian people is doomed
to fail; it will simply impose additional hardships upon the dispossessed Palestinian people and, of course, the host governments
whose contributions, direct and indirect, by far exceed those of any
other country in the world, not excluding the major powers.

What are the basic features of this trend?

(1) The total number of refugees is presently in excess of
1,800,000. Only 45% of this refugee population were in receipt of
Agency relief as of June 1980 because of a ceiling arrangement
introduced almost 20 years ago. The total refugee population is
well under half the Palestinian people.

(2) Even the basic rations to those most in need had been
reduced by half in 1979 and 1980 from 10 kg to 5 kg of flour per
month. Similar drastic cutbacks had been applied to the few other
components of basic rations, meagre as they are.

(3) Jordan's direct assistance to the refugees, in addition to contributions to U.N.R.W.A., amounted in the present fiscal year to
$35.5 million. This is in addition to catering to 250,000 displaced
persons from the West Bank for whom since 1967 the Jordan Government has been responsible. If we calculate the other common
services provided to the citizens, in addition to unfettered opportunities for gainful employment for those able to work, the amount
would vastly exceed the aforementioned figure.

(4) The Agency's priorities put education in the forefront and
laudably so, and the Agency devotes well over half its expenditure
to education and training, with over 314,000 children in its schools
and 4,700 trainees in its vocational and teacher-training centres.
The second priority is the Agency's health services. The third priority is the relief and welfare services.

(5) Since relief has been cut to the bone and, at all events, cannot

be reduced further because it is contributed in kind, and since the meagre health services have been miraculously kept intact, then the only avenue left for additional reduction is in the education programme which is its first priority.

In 1979 the secondary schooling was abandoned and the preparatory-cycle schools were substantially reduced and are now lingering on from month to month.

The Agency will go into 1981 with a budgetary deficit of $70.4 million without making any provision for the buying of flour. The budget for 1980 had been set at $200.3 million. The proposed budget for 1981 stands at $230.9 million. The figure increases in the targeted budgets do not in any way reflect higher services but simply a runaway inflation in goods and services which is presently encompassing the world.

On the contrary, the Agency has come to the conclusion that it would be less damaging to lay down financial responsibility for all its schools in Jordan and the Syrian Arab Republic, while maintaining its schools in Lebanon, the West Bank and Gaza. If the decision were taken to mutilate the school system throughout the whole area of operations, this system would then be permanently damaged, or at the least would take a long time to restore. Although as a desperate measure the Agency planned in 1979 to close the lower secondary cycle of education in all its five fields, this would have caused enormous administrative disruption because, apart from any other consideration, most of U.N.R.W.A.'s schools work on a double-shift basis whereby two schools share the same building at different times of the day. Should it prove necessary in 1981 to plan to reduce the health and education programmes, the Agency may decide to try to keep the programmes intact in certain fields while abandoning responsibility for them in others. The Agency would give priority to maintaining them in the occupied territories of the West Bank and Gaza, where there is so far no Arab government or administration which might be in a position to assume responsibility for the programmes.

It is inconceivable that a few hundred thousand children (young boys and girls) and thousands of qualified teachers should be thrown out of their classrooms into the streets. Yet now the Agency has reached a financial crisis where it is telling us that it would and could no longer take responsibility for the schooling of those children. Is this a fair deal when their usurper and tormentor, Israel,

over the past three and a half years received $10 billion in official
assistance from the U.S.A., let alone the billions of tax-exempt
contributions which are in reality contributions by a hard-pressed
American taxpayer?

The Palestinian people are one of the most hardworking, conscientious and proud people in the world. They would be the hap-
piest people on earth if the U.N.R.W.A. operations, which they
deeply appreciate, were to be terminated tomorrow – provided the
other part of the equation, namely implementation of their inalienable right of return to their homeland, were likewise and simultaneously to be fulfilled. But to leave the dispossessed Palestinians
in limbo, in their greatest hour of need, can only be described as a
crime against humanity, for which the powers which had wrought
this catastrophe upon them must bear the most colossal responsibility, ethically, morally and legally.[58]

12
U.N. Reports

The Exercise of the Inalienable Rights of the Palestinian People

When the General Assembly was seized of the question of Palestine in 1947 at the behest of the Mandatory Power, it acted without delay to form a committee, which became known as the United Nations Special Committee on Palestine (U.N.S.C.O.P.), to work out a solution of the question of Palestine. Though belatedly, the Committee on the Exercise of the Inalienable Rights of the Palestinian People has been set up and has become the equivalent of the original U.N.S.C.O.P., but with much more substantial support from the General Assembly It has judiciously, objectively and pragmatically sought ways and means to implement all the U.N. resolutions on the question, taking into consideration the practical changes which have taken place in the interim of 30 years. The Committee's pragmatism has extended to bending the rules by dividing the scheduling of implementation into phases, thereby discarding many of the strictures of the U.N. resolutions themselves. Thus priority is accorded, in phase one, to the return to their homes of the Palestinians displaced as a result of the war of June 1967. Twelve years have already elapsed and no action has been taken to carry it out. Phase two stipulates that the U.N., in cooperation with the States directly involved and with the P.L.O. as the interim representative of the Palestinian entity, should make the arrangements necessary to enable Palestinians displaced between

1948 and 1967 to exercise their right to return to their homes and property, or should provide compensation for those not choosing to return. Finally the Committee spells out the provisions concerning the right to self-determination and national independence subsequent to the evacuation of the territories occupied by force in violation of the principles of the Charter and relevant resolutions of the U.N.[38]

The Report ['The Question of Palestine'] gives full recognition to the fact that the passage of time and changed circumstances have diluted and undermined what an earlier generation of Palestinians would have viewed as truisms. Even as recently as 1949, many Palestinians felt that they had made their supreme concession by conceding to partition and to alienation of substantial portions of their country.

It is not an unadulterated pro-Palestinian instrument as the Israelis claim; nor is it anti-Israeli either in tone or in content, unless of course the Israelis' final aim is the total takeover of the whole of Palestine, and the throwing out of all the Palestinian people into the wilderness.

For the moment of truth has come when the Israelis have the burden and the responsibility to opt for peace – genuine peace – or to take the perilous road of indefinite conflict, extending for generations.

In concrete terms, and without the embellishments and references to the numerous U.N. resolutions on the Palestine issue, the Report gives pride of place to the following:

(1) Israel should withdraw from all the Arab territories occupied since 1967, in accordance with the principle of the inadmissibility of any acquisition of territories by the use of military force, and the relevant resolutions of the Security Council.

(2) The Palestinian people should be enabled to exercise its inalienable right to national self-determination, including the right to establish an independent State in Palestine, in accordance with the principles of the Charter of the U.N. Palestinian refugees wishing to return to their homes and to live in peace with their neighbours should have the right to do so, and those choosing not to return should receive compensation for their properties.

(3) A timetable should be established by the Security Council for the complete withdrawal by Israeli occupation forces from those areas occupied in 1967; such withdrawal should be completed no later than 1 June 1977.

(4) During an interim period and if deemed necessary, the Security Council could establish a temporary U.N. peacekeeping force in the region and provide formal assurances of security, so as to facilitate withdrawal by Israel from the occupied areas.

In another section the Report proposes additionally that the Security Council for the long run could provide international guarantees for the peace and security of all States and peoples in the Middle East.

(5) Foremost, in my delegation's judgement, is that Israel withdraw from the settlements already established since 1967 in the occupied territories, contrary to the provisions of the Fourth Geneva Convention, and in violation of the resolutions of the U.N. Israel should also desist from the establishment of new settlements in the occupied territories. This is uppermost because, if our reading of the Report is correct, the territorial delineation proposed for the Palestinians by the Committee is the West Bank and Gaza, a mere one-fifth of geographic Palestine under the British Mandate

(6) The Report, while setting out its programme of implementation in phases, as it must necessarily do in a situation so confounded by the passage of years and accumulation of one-sided reverses, nonetheless accords priorities and speedy action to a number of steps which can ill afford further delays. I have touched upon some of them and I shall now turn to one which, in my opinion, is pivotal to all. This expresses the belief that the prevailing situation in the Middle East should not be allowed to stagnate. We can shout our voices hoarse in debate, but to no avail. What is imperative is movement, and the view was expressed that there was a need to reconvene the Geneva Peace Conference on the Middle East, with the participation of all parties concerned, including the P.L.O., in order to deal with the problem in all its aspects. Let us all remember that what is envisaged is not an *ad hoc* agreement to resolve the consequences of the 1967 war. What is envisaged is a comprehensive, overall and lasting solution, in which all are agreed the Palestine question is central. It is in everybody's interest, including Israel's, that the Palestinians *per se* should participate. We know full well that the process of dialogue and negotiation will entail a great deal of give and take, of concession and counter-concession which only the Palestinians and the Israelis may be willing and able to make. Theirs is a fateful task which involves

future generations. Needless to say, they are the ones who, in the final analysis, will have to live side by side, in amity and normalcy.

I belong to a generation which has seen numerous reports and as numerous resolutions passed solemnly by the Assembly, the Security Council, and other organs of the U.N., only to go unheeded and unfulfilled. That is why the Palestinian people are in such a state of despair. Look back on practically all the issues which have appeared on the agenda of the Assembly during the past 30 years. In almost all cases they were either resolved and deleted from the agenda, or at least have moved, albeit slowly, forward towards being resolved. It is only when it comes to the question of Palestine and the Palestinians that we find ourselves up against an impenetrable wall, a process of retrogression instead of progression, where our people are losing more of their homeland, more of their lands, more of their rights, in short more of everything at an alarmingly accelerating rate. They will not be elated by paper victories, nor deterred by the immensity of the reverses to which they are continually being subjected.[6]

Israeli Practices affecting the Human Rights of the Population of the Occupied Territories

The Report, to Investigate Israeli Practices Affecting the Human Rights of the Population of the Occupied Territories, no longer portrays the ordeal of our people under occupation. The term 'practices', turned into malpractices, connotes irregular, illegal and brutal behaviour by the Israeli occupation authorities. A more appropriate title should be 'Israeli colonization and its concomitant threat to the survival of the Palestinian people under occupation'.

The issues at stake are far more serious than practices or malpractices, human rights, in the conventional sense, or their violation. These are terms which 13 years of Israeli occupation have rendered meaningless and inapplicable.[59]

The report is a balanced portrayal of three basic characteristics of Israeli practices in the occupied territories:

Firstly – and in political terms most importantly – is the policy of annexation and settlement. Although the U.N. Special Committee has been denied access to the occupied Arab territories, it nevertheless succeeded in producing maps which unmistakably illustrate the magnitude and extent to which Israeli annexation and settlement in the West Bank, Gaza, the Golan Heights and Sinai have reached, and they are alarming proportions indeed. Jerusalem and the heartland of the West Bank as a whole have been largely devoured. The greater part of the fertile Jordan valley west of the River Jordan has been sequestrated from its legitimate farmers and handed over to Israeli settlers. The deep hinterland of the West Bank, even the barren hills, have not been spared. Wherever there is a Palestinian city, town or village, the Israelis make a point of strangulating it, by building structures – ugly as they may be – overlooking it and/or encircling it. It is no exaggeration to state that the Israeli occupation authorities are devouring and annexing the territories occupied in 1967 with a deliberate zeal which far exceeds their absorption of the territories occupied in 1948 – both within and without the areas allotted to Israel under the partition resolution of 29 November 1947 – where any observer can see for himself large areas of the country unsettled, undeveloped and uninhabited. It is not, therefore, dearth of territory which motivates the plundering of Arab land in the occupied territories. The motivation is far more sinister and it is unquestionably a race by Israel against time, to render the continued presence of the Palestinians in the occupied territories virtually untenable. Have the designs of annexation, during 10 years of occupation, been fulfilled? The answer is a categorical *no*. This is not my own answer but is the definitive answer of the Special Committee pertaining to Israeli practices in the occupied territories. Lest the Israelis accuse the Committee of partiality as they have been prone to do in the past, the Committee derived its sources of information almost wholly from the official statements of policy, made continually by the leaders of Israel and all others who have a voice in the formulation and implementation of policy. The Israeli press in its turn has been giving detailed descriptions of the settlements already established, the settlements under construction and those being contemplated but still on the drawing-boards.

The Israeli practices in the occupied territories are multi-dimensional, but the most far-reaching in its implications is the policy of annexation.

The second point concerns the methods of acquisition of land in the occupied territories. The paragraph states that these methods may be classified into purchase, outright expropriation and expropriation with payment of compensation. Apart from a handful of crooks, agents and brokers who can be counted on the fingers of one's hands, there have been no voluntary sales of land or expropriations with payments of compensation. What happens is what happened in a plot of 25,000 square metres opposite the Ambassador Hotel in Sheikh Jarah Quarter, owned by at least 25 families; the Israeli authorities confiscate the land, and then send notices to the proprietors that compensation has been deposited in a bank. No one to my knowledge has ever accepted, or even considered accepting, compensation. In 99% of such cases, expropriation has been the dominant method, and compensation, whenever or wherever offered, was likewise categorically turned down by the people of the occupied territories.[7]

There are two dimensions to this situation: one is the habitat, mother-earth, geography, a homeland, a livelihood and everything else that goes with them; the second is the human being, the human element which inhabits the land. Both are inextricable, though it is difficult in the extreme to identify in this situation which is more catastrophic than the other.

Let me begin with the habitat. The Government of Jordan, private research centres, associations and others in Jerusalem, Amman and Beirut have made an on-the-spot compilation and breakdown of the magnitude of Israeli sequestration and colonization, district by district, in the tiny West Bank. Here are the results:

Part I: The Jerusalem district

(1) Atarot Colony, established in 1970 in the vicinity of Jerusalem airport (Qalandia). In the process, 10,000 dunums of land belonging to the inhabitants of Beit Hanina village were confiscated. An Israeli industrial complex comprising 61 factories was established on this land.

(2) Neve Ya'akov, established in 1973 near Beit Hanina to the north-east of the Jerusalem–Ramallah road. As a residential area the plan comprises the establishment of 4,000 housing units; 1,300 have been completed; work is under way to complete the remaining units. It is designed to house 17,000 colonizers. Again, over 10,000 dunums of land, the property of the inhabitants of Beit Hanina, were sequestrated. Up to the end of 1976 the Israeli colonizers numbered at least 10,000.

(3) Ramot, established in 1973 near Nebi Sumwail village to the north-west of Jerusalem on lands confiscated from the villages of Beit Iksa and Beit Hanina. The confiscated land amounted to 3,000

dunums. It presently comprises 1,500 housing units. Plans have been drawn up to build an additional 8,000 housing units to accommodate 35,000 Israeli colonizers. The Arab houses (at least 100) in the village of Nebi Sumwail were demolished, and the lands of the village were annexed to the Israeli colony. By the end of 1976, 2,400 colonizers had already been settled there.

(4) Ramat Eshkol, established in 1968 on the Mount Scopus area within Jerusalem. The area is 600 dunums, and links West to East Jerusalem; it comprises 1,700 housing units. The plan is for this quarter to expand to 2,200 housing units (1,850 flats in high-rise buildings, 350 houses of one or two floors). Israeli settlers in this quarter reached 7,000 by the end of 1976.

(5) The French Hill (known before 1967 as Karm Louis) in the north of Jerusalem. Established in 1969 to the east of Mount Scopus on the Jerusalem–Ramallah road. The area of Arab lands confiscated and on which this project was built is approximately 15,000 dunums. 5,000 housing units have been established and occupied. 350 additional housing units are under construction. The lands confiscated are the property of Palestinian landowners, the State of Jordan, the Latin Monastery, and a few individual Jewish proprietors who had acquired some dunums before 1948. The Israeli colonizers at this locality amounted to 8,500 at the end of 1976.

(6) Nahlat Dafna, established in the north of Jerusalem over 270 dunums of lands confiscated from several Arab families, including lands donated for the charitable foundation of the late Amina Khalidi. 1,400 housing units have been built with public facilities to serve 2,400 units, in anticipation of further expansion.

(7) Gilo, formerly the Arab suburb of Sharafaat, on elevated land one kilometre distant from the formerly divided Arab village of Beit Safafa, south of Jerusalem. 1,200 housing units have been constructed since 1973. The overall design is to expand the project to 10,000 housing units. Altogether, the occupation authorities have confiscated 4,000 dunums of land from their Palestinian proprietors. There are four phases to the project. When completed by 1980, it would house 35,000 Israeli colonizers. In 1976, the settlers numbered 4,800.

(8) East Talpiot, constructed in 1973 near the Abu Thur and Sur Bahir of the Jabal al Mukkabir area. The latter has been chosen as the location for the Israeli Government headquarters. The con-

struction is taking place over a huge area amounting to 20,000 dunums of confiscated Palestinian lands. It is three kilometres to the south of the Old City of Jerusalem.

(9) The Jewish Quarter in the Old City. It now encompasses an area extending between the Western Wall of the Aqsa Mosque to the Latin Monastery. Most of these lands are Islamic foundations, and parts are Arab property and Jewish property. The construction started in 1967 after demolishing 160 Arab houses, and the confiscation of 600 additional houses and the forcible expulsion up to 1977 of 6,500 Arab residents. 320 Israeli houses and a commercial centre have so far been built. The drawn-up plans provide for the construction of an additional 8,000 housing units.

(10) A vast expansion since 1969 of the Hebrew University of Mount Scopus, including housing projects, mostly on confiscated land. It should be recalled that after 1948 when Israel occupied four-fifths of Palestine they built an alternative Hebrew University on the lands and ruins of Ein Karem village, in the western suburbs of Jerusalem.

(11) San-Hediria extension. The expansion in this quarter started in 1973 where, up to 1975, 250 units had been built and many more arc not under construction. All the expansion has taken place on confiscated Palestinian lands.

(12) Elizariyah Village or the Mount of Olives, where the Israelis summarily confiscated 10,000 dunums of land for housing units. It is in the eastern sector of Arab Jerusalem.

Part II: Ramallah and Bireh district, 22 kilometres to the north of Jerusalem

(1) The Shilo colony, established in 1978 on confiscated Arab lands, from the villagers of Turmus 'Aya, Abu Falah and al-Mughir. The confiscated lands amounted to 1,500 dunums. The inhabitants of these villages have been forbidden entry to their lands to graze their livestock and utilize the water-wells upon which they have depended for centuries. The Shilo colony is agricultural, military and residential, of the Nahal type, and is affiliated to the Gush Emunim movement.

(2) Kochav Hashar, established in 1975 on confiscated Arab lands belonging to the two Palestinian villages of Dair Jreer and Kofr Malik. The area confiscated is 4,000 dunums. The intruding Israeli colony is of the Nahal type. Water has been drawn all the

way from Ein Samiyah spring, developed in the 1960s to meet the water crisis of Ramallah and Bireh towns.

(3) Ofra colony, established in 1975 on the Ramallah–Taybeh road, on 350 dunums of land belonging to the villagers of Ein Yabrud and Silwad, recognized by the Israeli occupation authorities on 26 July 1977. It is an affiliate of the Gush Emunim movement and is a Nahal military, as well as civilian, settlement. These colonies are in the very hinterland of the West Bank.

(4) and (5) Beit Horon–Canada Park, established in 1969, and the Canadian Park in 1976. The Gush Emunim colonizers joined in 1977. The two colonies were built on the ruins of three Arab villages, adjacent to the Latrun Monastery, namely Yalo, Emmuas and Beit Nuba. The three formerly prosperous villages were deliberately demolished by the Israeli army immediately after 1967. The dispersed inhabitants exceeded 4,000 although their sons and daughters working elsewhere number 10,000. The area confiscated is 16,000 dunums. One-fifth of the colonizers came from Britain, France, Romania and the U.S.A.

(6) Ramonim colony, to the north-east of the villages of Taybeh and Ramoun and to the north of the Ramallah–Jericho road. It also belongs to the Nahal military colonization. 300 dunums belonging to Taybeh villagers were confiscated.

(7) Bet El colony established adjacent to the Palestinian village of Bittin. In November 1977, 35 families were already housed as a vanguard for many more to come.

(8) Givon colony to the east of the Palestinian village of Jeeb in the Ramallah district. The colonists tried to force the villagers of Jeeb to refrain from planting their olive trees in the vicinity of the settlement, but failed. A number of new Jewish emigrants from Russia totalling 400 persons have joined this colony.

(9) Shilat, built in August 1977 on lands partly belonging to the Arab village of Midya and partly on what had after 1948 been no-man's-land in the Ramallah district.

(10) Nebi Saleh colony, colonized by two groups, one religious, the other non-religious. There are plans for its expansion and 400 dunums have been foreclosed and confiscated, although these are planted with olive trees, almonds and wheat.

(11) Shomron colony, near the Arab village of Deir Sharaf, in the Ramallah district, colonized in October 1977 by Gush Emunim. There are plans for its expansion.

Part III: The districts of Hebron and Bethlehem

(1) Kiryat Arba', established on 12 April 1968 at first without the occupation authorities' recognition, in and around the Park Hotel in Hebron. It is presently residential-industrial with a population of 1,500 living in 400 housing units. There are still 90 empty units awaiting new immigrants. It completely dominates the downtown area of the city of Hebron. 1,500 dunums of land were confiscated from the inhabitants of Hebron and Halhoul. Vine plantations and houses were destroyed in the process. Early in 1972 an industrial complex was added, and preparations are under way to create a tourist centre under the supervision of the Israeli Ministry of Industry and Commerce.

(2) Kfar Etzion, founded originally in 1934 under the British Mandate. Re-established immediately after the 1967 war, over 1,000 dunums of land. It is a *kibbutz* inhabited by a religious group and members of Hapoel Hamizrahi. Population 500, including 25% from France, Britain and South Africa and 23% from the U.S.A. I should point out here that even though this settlement, as well as Neve Yacoub, existed prior to 1948, the Geneva Convention forbids any changes in the occupied territories, pending a final settlement.

(3) Yittir, established in 1977 by the Gush Emunim colonists. The new settlement is located to the north of the two Arab villages of Yatta and Samou. The latter village, you will recall, was subjected to a massive Israeli attack in 1966 and was rebuilt before the 1967 war. 1,700 dunums of land were confiscated from the two villages to build the Yettir settlement in 1977.

(4) and (5) Rosh Tzurin and Alan Shvot. Both colonies were built in 1969 near Kfar Etzion on the Jerusalem–Hebron road. The lands on which the two settlements were built are the property of the two Arab villages of Irtass and Nahalin. The settlers are followers of the Mifdal religious party. The lands confiscated amount to 8,000 dunums and the 1,500 colonizers came from South Africa, the U.S.A. and Israel.

(6) Migdal Oz, established in 1978, over confiscated and foreclosed lands, approximately 2,000 dunums, belonging to the Arab village of Beit Ummar.

(7) Efrat, under construction since 1977 as a *kibbutz*.

(8) El Azar, established in 1975 on the Hebron–Jerusalem road on lands confiscated from al-Khader Arab village. It belongs to the

Moshaaf category and comprises Jewish families from Canada, Britain and the U.S.A. It comprises chemical as well as electronic manufacture.

(9) Tekoah, established to the south of Bethlehem over 3,000 dunums of confiscated land, property of 50 Palestinian families in the village of Rafidi, in the Bethlehem area.

(10) Ma'Ale Adumin, established in 1972 near the red plains of Khan el-Ahmar on the Jerusalem–Jericho road. The amount of lands confiscated is a staggering 70,000 dunums, by the standards of the tiny West Bank. The lands belong to the three Arab villages of Essawiyah, Eizariyah and Abu Dees. An industrial town has been constructed in this area, astride the main road between Jerusalem and Amman. There is also a plan to settle 2,500 Israeli workers on the location.

(11) Dahriya, established by the Hashomer Hatzaer Nahal around the police station in the Palestinian village of Dhahiriya, in the Hebron district. It was established in October 1977 inside the green line, on the Hebron–Beer Sheba road.

Part IV: The Nablus–Tulkarm–Jenin towns

(1) Kaddum (Elon Morea), established on the main road linking the city of Nablus and the town of Qalqilia. It will be recalled that in the aftermath of the 1967 war, the Israeli military inflicted extensive demolitions on this town. Kaddum was built on 300 dunums of confiscated land belonging to the inhabitants of the Arab village of Kofr Qaddum. The Jewish settlers came from Israel, Britain, South Africa, the U.S.A. and the U.S.S.R.

(2) Mekora, established on 28 December 1972 on 4,000 dunums of lands confiscated from the two Arab villages of Beit Dajan and Beit Fureek. Originally Nahal, subsequently made into the Moshaf type. Two water reservoirs have been constructed, one to water the existing lands, the second to cater to further confiscated lands and expansion.

(3) Gittit, established in August 1972 on 5,000 dunums of confiscated Palestinian lands belonging to the village of Aqraba, in the Nablus district. The settlers are followers of the Herut party of Begin. It should be noted here that the Arab village of Aqraba had been a victim of an ugly attack on 28 April 1973, when Israeli planes sprayed large areas of cultivated land with poisonous chem-

icals during the harvest season. The occupation authorities then confiscated the village lands on 'security grounds'.

(4) Mes'ha Pe'erim, established in April 1977 on lands confiscated from the Arab village of Mes'ha. Shlomo Efni, a senior official of the Israeli Ministry of Housing, stated in May 1977 that his Ministry was planning further expansion at the expense of Mes'ha village by building 500 new housing units.

(5) Malki Shua, established in 1976 on lands confiscated from the Arab village of Fakkua, north of the town of Jenin.

(6) Haris colony, established near the Arab village of Kofr Haaris in 1978, in the Nablus district over 500 dunums of confiscated land belonging to the two Arab villages of Haaris and Silfeet.

(7) Silat Edahar, established in January 1978 on lands confiscated from the Arab village of Seelat Edadhr.

(8) Tapuah, established in 1978 on lands confiscated from the Arab village of Yassuuf.

(9) Sa Nur or Dotan, established in November 1977 in the Jenin area on Arab lands confiscated in the vicinity of a former police headquarters.

(10) Karne Shomron, established near the Arab village of Jensafuut in the Tulkarm district.

(11) Reinhan, established near Khirbet lower Ein es-Sahla' in Jenin. It is a Nahal.

(12) Kofr Sur or Salit, established early in 1978 on 1,300 dunums of land, confiscated from the villagers of Kofr Suur.

Part V: The Jordan Valley

(1) Mehola, established in 1968 on the Beisan–Jiftlek–Toubas road over 6,400 dunums of confiscated land. It should be pointed out that as a consequence of drilling water-wells for this and other settlements throughout the Jordan valley, the water-wells of the Arab farmers have dried up and many of the citrus, banana and vegetable plantations have been ruined, in violation of all norms of international law. In one area, only two citrus farms have so far been spared this brutal destruction; this normally represents a lifelong effort of toil and investment.

(2) Nahal Ro'I, established in 1976 on lands confiscated from the villagers of Toubaas, over 800 dunums.

(3) Beka'ot, established in June 1972 on 5,000 dunums of

confiscated lands belonging to the villages of Tammoun, Khirbet Umm el-Qutton and Qirbet Moufia. The occupation authorities have also foreclosed 1,800 additional dunums from Buqai'ah esh-Shamaliya.

(4) Hamra, established in May 1971 on the Nablus–Jisr Ramy road. 10,000 dunums of the most fertile lands of the villages of Wadi el-Far'ah and Beit Dajan were confiscated as well as 600 dunums from the Jifflek village.

(5) Ma'Ale Ephraim, established in 1972 on the Aqraba–Fasael road.

(6) Patza'el, on 3,000 dunums of confiscated lands belonging to the village of Fasayel, established in December 1970.

(7) Tomer, established in 1976 to the north of Fasayel.

(8) Gilgal, established in November 1969 13 kilometres north of Jericho. Built on 3,300 dunums of sequestrated lands.

(9) Netiv Hagdud, established to the north of Gilgal in 1976.

(10) Na'Aran, established in December 1970 to the east of the Arab village of 'Uojah. The confiscated lands amount to 20,000 dunums of cultivable lands. It is an affiliate of the Labour Party.

(11) Yitav, established in 1970 on 2,700 dunums of lands belonging to the two Arab villages of Lower and Upper 'Uoja.

(12) Al-Mog, established in February 1968 on the Jericho–Dead Sea–Jerusalem road, recognized by the occupation in 1974 and renamed Yehuda el-Mog.

(13) Kalia, before 1948 a small Israeli settlement, built in 1968 near the Dead Sea, and drawing water from the Wadi el-Qilt water resource.

(14) Mitzpe Shalem, established in December 1970 between Kalia and Ein Giddi on the Dead Sea, to the south of al-Fashka Arab lands and water resource.

(15) Argaman, established at the terminal of the Nablus–Damya bridge, on 5,000 dunums of land belonging to the Arab village of Marj Na'ja. The five artesian wells of the village were also confiscated.

(16) Masuah, established in November 1969 on the Hartaba plateau on 4,000 dunums of lands confiscated from the Giftlek farmers.

(17) New Massuah, planned in 1977 to become the central occupation city, to supervise the total colonization of the Jordan valley. Built on 800 dunums of lands confiscated from the 'Ajaarjra village

which Israel had destroyed after 1967 and forcibly expelled its 5,000 inhabitants, including the 'Ajaarja, al-Waheedat, al-Jubairat, and Ihdiwaad al-Masaaeed. Jiftlik village had likewise been destroyed after the occupation in 1967 and its 2,000 inhabitants dispersed.

(18) Mevsan, under construction since 1977. It will be renamed No. 165 because it is 165 metres below sea level.

Even the philanthrophic society of Mr Musa al-Alami Mashruu'al-Insha'i' for the orphaned in the Jericho area has been 90% confiscated and its 18 wells either taken over or demolished. Lord Home, a former British Prime Minister, and other world dignitaries interceded personally, but their efforts fell on deaf ears. I happen to be a member *in absentia*, because of the occupation, of the Board of Trustees of this purely humanitarian project to rehabilitate and educate generations of orphaned Palestinian children who have no other means of support.

The avalanche of colonization continuous unabated as we read our daily papers and reports. Indeed, it is now the publicly acknowledged policy of the Israeli Government. They regard it as praiseworthy flexibility when they reluctantly concede that they may accept a three-month moratorium on building new settlements, and suggest instead a strengthening of existing ones. The truth is that, unlike all other countries in the world where people come and build towns and villages, the Israelis confiscate the lands, build towns and settlements on other people's land and await the arrival of new immigrants to strengthen the settlements and build new ones. The only limitation on them is the lack of sufficient people to dislodge and displace the indigenous inhabitants.

I know the villages, towns and locations inside out, not only because I am a part of them, but also because I had served in the mid-1950s as Chairman of the Jordanian delegation to the Mixed Armistice Commission, which duty took me to every part of the land. I can state without the slightest hesitation that Israeli colonization has spared hardly a single area which can be identified as having any means of sustenance, particularly water and cultivable land, even though the West Bank is the least endowed of the regions of Palestine.

The truth is that colonization is a prelude to the expulsion of the Palestinian people either directly or indirectly. And this in turn is a prelude to expansion and aggression against the neighbouring

Arab countries. As a proof of the priority which the Israelis attach to colonization, there are currently six Israeli ministries with direct or indirect jurisdiction over colonization. These are in addition to the activities of most parties affiliated to the World Zionist Congress and the Jewish Agency. Former Israeli Minister Galeeli declared in one of his statements:

I have been brought up and inculcated with the conviction that the West Bank and the shores of the Mediterranean up to al-'Areesh are my historical homeland. And not a homeland in spirit or history or books, but as a space for a factual ingathering for the Zionist movement by means of colonization. Whoever thinks that the Zionist movement would consider giving up, or refraining from colonization, in the Jordan valley, a unified Israeli Jerusalem and elsewhere, our answer is: we establish colonies not to give them up, but to include them within the boundaries of Israel. There is no decision to close any area to colonization.

This was stated in the *Jerusalem Post* as far back as 25 September 1967.

What are the overall implications of this Zionist onslaught? First and foremost: to turn the Palestinian people inside the occupied territories into drawers of water and hewers of wood, in other words slave-lavour, as Israel did to the remnants of the Palestinian people who remained there after 1948, and 90% of whose lands have been confiscated.[24]

By 1979, 27% of the occupied West Bank and Jerusalem had already been devoured, and the process was continuing relentlessly. Upwards of 90,000 Israelis had settled in 'expanded Jerusalem' and the rest of the West Bank; the Palestinian population had decreased since 1967 by a staggering 32%; the water resources had been effectively seized by the occupation authorities. The new data accumulated by Jordan shows that Israel is helping itself to five-sixths of the water resources of the West Bank for the illicit settlements in the West Bank as well as for the substantially expanded and therefore illegitimate Israel of 1948–9. What is left to the Palestinians is a mere 100 million cubic metres out of a total of approximately 850 million cubic metres. I need hardly add that without water life itself becomes impossible.

It should never be overlooked that the West Bank is a tiny 4,800 square kilometres, mostly mountainous. Every inch of land, every drop of water confiscated from the Palestinians is for them a matter of survival. And yet, just to recount some of the confiscations in the months of August and September 1979 we have the following pattern:

On 29 August 1979 Radio Israel announced that the occupation authorities have decided to establish four new settlements near the Arab town of Qalqilya.

On 30 August *Al-Sha'b* reported that work on the establishment of four new colonies in the West Bank would be commenced within the next few days. Two settlements will be in the Jericho area and two will be near Karne Shamron in the Nablus district. The levelling of land had already started for the establishment of a new settlement to the east of Jerusalem, to be named Ma'ale Adumim B. The new four settlements will be named Reihan B, Reihan C, Karne Shamron C and Karne Shamron D.

On 3 September 1979, the Israeli authorities stated that colonizers at the Ofra settlements, near the Arab village of Ein Yabroud to the north-east of Ramallah, have seized large areas of land belonging to the village. This settlement, established seven years ago, is 10 kilometres from Ramallah.

On the same day, work on a new settlement named Gani Lahal, north-west of Khan Yunis in the Gaza Strip, had begun. This will be the fourth within a complex of seven settlements to separate Egypt and the Gaza Strip.

On 9 September, *Ma'ariv*, the Israeli daily, reported that the occupation authorities had decided to establish 30 new settlements in Western Galilee, 17 of which will be made ready to accommodate settlers within three months, while the 13 others will be ready to accommodate settlers by May 1980.

On 10 September an Israeli Ministerial Committee approved the establishment of four new settlements in the Nablus district. It was also reported that the settlements department of the Jewish Agency had drawn up plans to establish a chain of setlements with a view to surrounding the city of Nablus as a top priority, including settlements in the heart of the Nablus mountains in Kadomim, Gosh Elan Moreh, Gosh Isri Shamron. The major objective, it was stressed, was to consolidate control of the West Bank and create a new *fait accompli* before the end of the so-called self-rule talks.

The World Zionist Organization Master Plan for the development of settlements in the West Bank of Jordan for the period 1979–83, and a 20-year plan (1975–95) are presently under implementation. These secret plans have been edited by Matityahu Drobles; it is most significant to cite the introduction to the Plan, especially for the first five years as it had been drawn after the Camp David Accords and coincides with the same period, considered to be transitional in those Accords. It clearly shows the overall designs of the Zionists to the future of the west Bank.

For some considerable time now, the lack has been felt of a comprehensive, well-founded and professional plan of settlement of Judea and Samaria. Therefore, upon my assumption of the post of head of the Jewish Agency's land settlement department and head of the rural settlement department of the World Zionist Organization, I began with the help of the first-rate and highly experienced staff in the department to seek out various possibilities for the consolidation of a general Master Plan in Judea and Samaria whose implementation would extend, in the first stage, five years. At the centre of this examination stands a comprehensive and systematic land survey. When the survey is completed, it is probable that we will be able to plan the disposition of settlements additional – I repeat, additional – to those proposed below. The following are the principles which guided the Plan:

(1) Settlement thoughout the entire land of Israel is for security and by right. A strip of settlements at strategic sites enhances both internal and external security alike, as well as making concrete and realizing our right to Eretz-Israel. . .

(3). . . The disposition of the settlements must be carried out not only *around* the settlements of the minorities [meaning the indigenous Palestinians] but also in between them, this is in accordance with the settlement policy adopted in Galilee and in other parts of the country.

Therefore, the proposed settlement blocs are situated at a strip surrounding the Judea and Samaria ridge – starting from its western slopes from south to north – both between the minorities population and around it.

To dispel any doubt that the Master Plan represents the official policy of the Israelis, I quote from the Introduction the following:

> As is known, it is the task of the land settlement department to initiate, plan and implement the settlement enterprise, according to the decisions of the Government of the Joint Government World Zionist Organization Committee for Settlement.

These are not the words of Gush Emunim but of the Israeli Government, in collaboration with the World Zionist Organization. The end result is so gruesome that the population of the occupied territories are referred to as 'minorities' in their own homeland as an annexed part of a yet greater Israel, and stripped of practically all the arable lands, water and other resources. They would be turned into a floating workforce for Israeli colonialism, or made to leave if they cannot tolerate it.

The term 'Israeli practices' has been invalidated by criminal plans, far exceeding practices or malpractices. The response of the international community should be no less than the magnitude of the challenge and the policies which are publicly being pursued and designed.

It is only fitting that in my discussion of the Israeli aggression in the occupied territories I should refer to the fate of occupied Jerusalem since the 1967 war. A brief compilation made by the Royal Commission on Jerusalem between 1967 and the beginning of 1979 reports:

General conditions in Occupied Jerusalem

After the 1967 war, the Israeli occupation authorities adopted a different approach towards Arab Jerusalem as compared to the rest of the West Bank, Gaza and other occupied Arab territories. For the latter territories, the establishment of Israeli settlements was the mechanism towards imposing a *de facto* situation, while in Arab Jerusalem, a *de jure* situation was initated, to be actively followed up by confiscating Arab lands and property and establishing Israeli settlements.

Motivated by the Zionist philosophy which continues to resort to such myths as the 'Promised Land', the Temple and Mount Zion, the Knesset passed a law, on 28 June 1967, extending the Israeli legal and administrative jurisdiction to include Arab Jerusalem. This illegal annexation is in violation of the fourth Geneva Convention and was condemned by U.N. General Assembly resolutions 2253 on 4 July 1967 and 2254 on 14 July 1967. Likewise, it was condemned by Security Council resolutions 252 on 21 May 1968 and 267 on 3 July 1969, and U.N.E.S.C.O. resolution of 10 October 1969. Nevertheless, the annexation law was utilized by Israel as the effective instrument to undertake a series of illegal measures aimed at the Israelization of Arab Jerusalem and the encirclement of the Arab presence demographically, culturally and economically.

These actions came to confirm the previous Zionist and Israeli prophecies and intentions which were expressed by Hertzel [the leading Zionist articulator, 1860–1904], David Ben Gurion [the founder of the State of Israel, 1886–1973], and Levi Eshkol [ex-Prime Minister of Israel]. Hertzel said in the First Zionist Congress of 1879: 'If one day we had Jerusalem and I were still living and capable of doing anything, I would erase everything not holy to the Jews and demolish all antiquities that have been there for centuries.'

A well-known statement of Ben Gurion is the following: 'There is no meaning for Palestine without Jerusalem, and no meaning for Jerusalem without the temple.'

On 17 June 1967 Eshkol said that: 'Israel will never leave the Old City of Jerusalem and shall work towards its natural and real limits.'

In the following, Israeli actions to settle in Arab Jerusalem, contain its population and shatter their demographic and cultural unity are presented briefly. Israel intends to create new realities in Arab Jerusalem which makes it appear impossible to change under any prospective political settlement.

(1) Demolition of Arab homes and properties

After the annexation of Arab Jerusalem, Israel demolished Arab homes in three-quarters in the Old City, namely Al-Sharaf, Bab Al-Silsilah and Harat Al-Maqharbah (Dung Gate). Their Arab inhabitants were forced to leave Old Jerusalem, a fact that met a number of Israeli objectives:

(a) to reduce the Arab population presence in the Old City as a first step and in the remaining parts of Arab Jerusalem later on;

(b) to create room in Arab Jerusalem sufficient to settle a substantial number of Israelis in the south-western part of the Old City. In addition, thousands of Jewish immigrants were settled in the high-rise residential buildings which encircled Arab Jerusalem;

(c) to create new realities in Arab Jerusalem, both physically and demographically, which complicate any possible implementation of the U.N. resolutions on Jerusalem.

The number of Arab homes and properties that were demolished in Al-Sharaf quarter alone were 1,215 houses, 427 shops and a girls' school.

(2) Land confiscation for Israeli settlements

The confiscation of Arab lands was a prerequisite for the establishment of Israeli settlements and Jewish residential quarters in Arab Jerusalem. For that purpose, the Israeli occupation authorities used a number of mechanisms, most of which were also used in the rest of the West Bank. These mechanisms are:

(a) confiscation of Arab lands on the basis of the Israeli law on 'absentee ownership'. All Arab inhabitants who were not present in Arab Jerusalem during or after the 1967 war are treated as 'absentee persons'. Moreover, Arab Palestinians who owned land and property in Jerusalem but resided in other parts of the West Bank were also considered as 'absentee owners'. Even in the so-called unified Jerusalem, inhabitants in Arab Jerusalem were considered by Israel as 'absentee owners' and treated as tenants in their own homes and lands.

(b) confiscation of Arab lands after declaring them 'restricted areas' for alleged security and military needs. This mechanism was used by Israel to confiscate 70,000 dunums in Beit Sahour and about 100,000 dunums in Khan Ul-Ahmar, which are both located in the area which will comprise the so-called Greater Jerusalem, according to Israeli projections. The usual procedure is to estalish military settlements in these areas which are transformed in due time to civilian settlements.

(c) in some cases, Arab lands were confiscated for alleged 'public uses' but were used afterwards for Israeli settlements.

(d) in accordance with the Israeli law for land expropriation in case of emergency the Israeli occupation authorities can confiscate any real estate in Arab Jerusalem for any of several reasons, such as public security, urgent public utilities, absorption of new immigrants, recreation of retired soldiers and others.

(e) Israel attempted also to secure legal evidence for its confiscation of Arab lands and properties in West Jerusalem seized by Israel in 1948 by offering compensation. However, the Arab inhabitants refused to receive such compensation, insisting on their rights of ownership.

(f) additional mechanisms were also used by the Israeli occupation authorities such as forgeries and the declaration of certain areas as 'green zones'.

As a result of the Israeli policy of settlement, a total area of 94,000 dunums of Arab lands was confiscated, restricted or fenced in Arab Jerusalem proper and its suburbs. Nine Jewish residential quarters and seven Israeli settlements were established in these areas. The nine Jewish residential quarters are:

(i) Ramat Ashkoul, established on Arab lands confiscated in Sheikh Jarrah and Sho'fat and comprising about 1,800 housing units. Its ultimate design provides for the settlement of 30,000 Jewish settlers.

(ii) Geba't Hamftar, established on Al-Thakhirah (French) hill in Sheikh Jarrah.

(iii) Shabera, established north of Sheikh Jarrah towards the Mount of Olives where residences for the Hebrew University and Hadassa hospital were built.

(iv) Neve Yaacob, established on lands confiscated in Beit Hanina and Hizma, and aimed at building 4,550 housing units.

(v) Atarout, an industrial area built on lands confiscated in Qalandiya.

(vi) Gelo, established on lands of Sharafat and Beit Safafa south of Jerusalem and comprising 9,000 housing units.

(vii) Mezrah Telbuut, established on al-Mukkabber mountain south of Jerusalem and comprising 2,000 housing units.

(viii) Anata, established on the Arab lands of Anata village north-east of Jerusalem with a total area of 3,000 dunums and including 1,200 housing units.

(ix) The Jewish Quarter in the Old City of Arab Jerusalem, where four Arab quarters were confiscated and their buildings and properties demolished.

In addition to these nine established Israeli residential suburbs, new ones are under construction for which Arab lands have been confiscated or restricted in Sour Baher, Abou Deis and Eizeriah.

The implanting of an Israeli quarter in the Old City of Jerusalem and the construction of high-rise residential buildings outside of the Old City encircling Arab Jerusalem clearly illustrate the Israeli mutilations which have altered the physical character of Arab

Jerusalem. Demographically, it led to the fragmentation of the Arab community and the shattering of its unity. Available figures indicate that between 1967 and 1978, about 76,600 Israelis settled in Arab Jerusalem while the Arab population decreased from 96,000 to 78,000, due to expulsion of the inhabitants.

(3) Education and culture

After the illegal annexation of Arab Jerusalem, Israel took the following measures relating to the education system:

(a) the cancellation of the existing Jordanian curriculum and the imposition of the Israeli curriculum which was taught in Arab schools in Israel after 1948. The imposed curriculum is based on the Israeli educational philosophy which, *inter alia,* conveys to Arab students that Palestine is a Jewish land and creates a sense of frustration and undermines the Arab culture and heritage.

(b) the closure of the Ministry of Education Office in Jerusalem and the control of the educational system by the Municipality of Jerusalem (at the secondary level).

(c) Israel cancelled 19 textbooks and subjected 59 others to revisions and omissions, particularly textbooks of religion, literature, history, geography and civic education.

(d) the Hebrew language was introduced as a requirement at the elementary level.

(e) a course on Israeli society and civic education replaced the course on Arab society that was taught prior to 1967.

(f) Arab students in Jerusalem were not permitted to enrol in other West Bank schools.

(g) after the 1967 war, the Israeli censor prohibited the circulation of 1,188 books and continued to refuse the entry of books and publications dealing with Arab culture and history. In the meantime, films and literature which are anathema to the values of Arab society were encouraged.

(h) Israel strove to weaken the sense of belonging and community among Arab inhabitants by discouraging social, cultural and sports activities.

(4) Civil and Islamic law

On 7 June 1967, the Israeli occupation authorities cancelled Arab courts in Jerusalem and transferred the Court of Appeals to

Ramallah. Accordingly, the Arab inhabitants of Jerusalem were left with no option but to resort to Israeli courts.

Israel required Arab lawyers and employees to submit application forms to the Israeli Minister of Justice, thus ending the judicial law prevailing in Arab Jerusalem and attaching it to Israeli law. The Arab lawyers refused to appear before the Israeli civil and military courts, declaring their objection to Israeli actions. Since then, Arab lawyers have refrained from practising law in Jerusalem during the past 12 years. As for the Shari'a Court in Jerusalem, the Israeli authorities did not accept documents and papers issued by it. Arab inhabitants of Jerusalem had to refer for initiation or certification of such documents to the Shari'a Court in Jaffa which falls under the jurisdiction of the Israeli Ministry of Religion. Bearing in mind that Shari'a courts deal with matters of personal status including marriage, divorce, alimony, inheritance, maintenance and guardianship, this action created many complications and civil problems for the Arab inhabitants.

(5) Desecration of Muslim and Christian Holy Places

In line with the Zionist precept that Jerusalem is the capital of an exclusively Jewish State, Israel attempted to destroy and distort living witnesses and manifestations of the Muslim and Christian heritage and holy shrines such as:

. . . (g) the Israeli occupation authorities renamed streets and sites in Arab Jerusalem of great religious and historic significance to the Arab and Muslim peoples. Bab Al-Magharbah, Al-Sharaf hill, Tariq al-Wad and Tariq al-Frere were given the Hebrew names of Rehab Beiti Mahsi, Geba't Hamftar, Rahob Hakai and Ha'im, respectively. In contrast, official U.N. records of 1949 show that the Arab governments of Egypt, Jordan, Lebanon and Syria solemnly undertook to guarantee the protection of and free access to the Holy Places, religious buildings and sites of Palestine situated in the territory placed under their authority by the final settlement of the Palestine problem or, pending that settlement, in the territory at present occupied by them under armistice agreements. Free access was declared to all pilgrims and visitors without discrimination as to nationality or faith. Thus, contrary to the Israeli allegations, Israelis and Jews were permitted access to the Holy Places, including the Wailing Wall. As the U.N. records show, it

was the Israeli Government which, for its own reasons, opted to
refuse making a similar declaration.

(6) Integration of Arab Jerusalem into the Israeli economy

The above measures were supplemented by actions that aimed at
the integration of Arab Jerusalem into the Israeli economy and its
isolation from the rest of the West Bank by the establishment of
customs posts around the city and the absorption of the Arab
economy into that of Israel by closing Arab banks and appropriat-
ing their funds, and exchanging Jordanian currency for Israeli currency, which latter dropped in value in an unprecedented manner –
from seven Israeli pounds to one Jordanian dinar to £160 to one
dinar – affecting the buying power of those Arabs who were compelled to use it. The Israeli occupation authorities implemented the
Israeli income-tax system on the Arab population, including the
added defence tax to be raised from the Arab population in the
interest of the Israeli defence forces occupying their land; the effect
of these measures on the Arab economy and the continued evacuation of Jerusalem citizens to the East Bank and other Arab countries was the first achievement of the Israeli occupations
authorities' plan in the occupied territories.[44]

13
The Begin 'Peace Plan' and the Camp David Accords

The following are some reasons why the Arab World has rejected the Begin 'Peace Plan' outright:

(1) It is a *de facto* perpetuation and legalization of the existing *status quo* of military occupation, masquerading under a deceptive and, to the world, a more palatable term of autonomy or self-rule. It would maintain its military occupation of the Arab sector of Jerusalem, the rest of the West Bank and the Gaza Strip. Under the plan, Israel would continue to assume responsibility, not only for 'external security' but also for internal police duties.

A few military governors would presumably lose the dubious glamour of being called military governors. But they would continue to assume the powers of such positions under a different guise. The mayors, of course, would continue to take care of the water systems, sewage and other municipal functions which they are doing already. But what military governor would want to do that in the first place?

(2) Israel would continue to exercise 'veto power' over the repatriation of Palestinians from their dispersal, including the close to one million inhabitants of Arab Jerusalem, the West Bank and the Gaza Strip, who have become displaced persons since 1967, let alone the 1.75 million Palestinian refugees who would be completely left out in the wilderness of their diaspora. The rights of those victimized people for repatriation or compensation are covered by U.N. resolution 194, which was introduced by the

United States in 1949 and which is sponsored and reiterated every
year by the U.S.A. and passed unanimously by the General
Assembly.

(3) The 'Administrative Council' proposed under the self-rule
plan would have no jurisdiction or authority over Israeli settlers
who have already colonized the heartland of East Jerusalem and
the West Bank. Thus, the Israeli settlers in those areas would enjoy
extraterritorial privileges which may have belonged to the age of
colonialism but are totally anathema in the post-decolonization of
the present era.

Thus, the Palestinian plight is reduced by a single stroke to
municipal autonomy in one small segment of 1948 mandated Palestine, and to one small portion of the Palestinian people.

Why this plan? In all likelihood, to disenfranchise the 1.1 million
Palestinian Arabs from the mainstream of life – by offering them an
option of acquiring Jordanian or Israeli citizenship without Jordan
even being present to offer or withhold such citizenship. To cordon
off those people into reservations, complete the colonization of their
territories until such time as life becomes so untenable and oppressive that the Palestinian inhabitants either vanish by natural attrition or are forced, by various means, to leave their ancestral homeland.

Theoretically, Palestinians of the occupied territories would be
able under the self-rule plan to settle in Israel and Israelis in East
Jerusalem, the West Bank and Gaza. But ask any Palestinian about
this seemingly generous offer and he will tell you it is devoid of
meaning. For they know that practically all lands in Israel are
either state domain and therefore inalienable, or are in the ownership of the Karen Kaymet, the Histadrut and other arms of the
State of Israel. In the fertile triangle plains which were taken over
by Israel in 1949 and where the inhabitants remained, Israel
confiscated 90% of their lands. Being resilient, high-quality farmers, one of them told a West Banker: 'If only we were allowed not to
take back but to purchase back the 90% confiscated from us, we
could buy our lands back with the proceeds of two to three years of
the 10% which has been left to us.' The same applies to Galilee and
elsewhere.

Peace could be achieved within 24 hours, with details to be
worked out in due course among the parties – if the Israeli leadership terminates its agonizing over the question of 'Israel' or 'imper-

ial Israel'. Are they willing to live and let live, or are they not? Armaments will never give a final answer to this tragic and potentially catastrophic dilemma. What gives the answer is a fundamental reappraisal of Israel's innermost attitude.

As for Jordan, the familial relationships between the people on both sides of the River Jordan render it inconceivable that the Jordan Government, the P.L.O. and the masses of the Jordanian and Palestinian people would countenance a suicidal separation. The two sides will have to sit down and agree on a meaningful and acceptable legal framework. Jordan has consistently insisted that Palestinians must exercise the right to self-determination under U.N. supervision.

It might be the wise course, in the meantime, to establish forthwith a U.N. interim administration, for a couple of years, during which the Palestinians will be able to establish their provisional institutions, pending a plebiscite. An additional five-year Israeli rule with licence for additional colonization will leave little territory indeed worth talking about, let alone the devastating impact of five additional years of occupation. A consciousness and application of peace is totally contrary to a consciousness of war, fear of war, and perpetual enmity. Most of the Arab World, including the Palestinians, have opted for a durable peace. The Israeli leadership evidently has not. Until it does, let us forget about peripheral and side issues and leave it to the future to resolve the issue. Everybody in the world has become tired of beating about the bush. Let us not compound their agony by repetitious argumentation.[20]

History is the long and tragic story of the fact that aggressors seldom give up their aggression voluntarily. The brutal truth is that the Zionists had long ago decided not to redeem any inalienable rights of the Palestinian people; they are determined to continue their policy of systematic despoliation and colonization of the 1967 conquered lands as they had done with the 1948 Palestinian lands, and to strangulate the remaining inhabitants to the point where the Palestinians' only option is to fade away or be banished. This is not my construction of the situation; it is the officially declared policy and practice of the Israelis. To mislead the world, they base their occupation and colonization on spurious, so-called security grounds!

Notwithstanding these incontestable facts, the U.S.A. and, stunningly, valiant Egypt and Israel signed full-fledged peace treaties, over the heads and without the knowledge or consent of the Palestinian people, the Arab parties concerned, the non-alignment movement and the U.N. which holds the Palestine question in trust.[40]

The Camp David Accords electrified large numbers of people as the be-all and end-all of resolving the perennial and intractable Middle East conflict and ushering in the millennium. Without entering into intentions or motivations, or even disparaging any and all efforts at achieving the long-elusive, just and lasting peace to which all people of goodwill aspire, it has been conclusively apparent to all those well-versed in the Arab–Israeli conflict and, more specifically, the Palestinian–Israeli conflict that the Accords simply side-tracked the core issue, namely the fate and survival of the Palestinian people in their ancestral homeland.

It was simply a rehash of the earlier Begin plan, designed not to give redemption to the 1.1 million Palestinians in Jerusalem and the rest of the West Bank and the Gaza Strip, but rather addressed to an Israeli dilemma of what to do to further separate and contain those inhabitants, without impinging upon the exclusive Jewish character of the Israeli State. Hence, the concept of civil rule or autonomy which the Camp David Accords provide for. Israeli military occupation would be perpetuated with a few cosmetic changes to convey the all too transparent impression that it has been terminated, except for what are called security and military considerations.[29]

The Camp David Accords – as far as the 1967 war or the Palestine question are concerned – do not conform to either Security Council resolutions 242 and 338 nor to the original General Assembly resolutions. There is no provision for military withdrawal; there is no provision for Palestinian national existence. There is no proposal for local self-government for the inhabitants as temporary residents and with no jurisdiction over their fate, resources, land, water, repatriation or anything to redeem the Palestinian people.[37]

The Israeli authorities under the Accords would not agree to military withdrawal, even after the proposed five-year interim period; they would retain overall authority, even in matters pertaining to internal security; they would not concede sovereignty ever over the substantially dwarfed and colonized occupied Palestinian lands, earmarked as a homeland for the Palestinian people.

The Israelis insist on going ahead with their unrestricted and relentless policy of expropriation and colonization which has already devoured 29% of the occupied lands and has rendered any talk about a Palestinian homeland a sham.

They have insisted on retaining a veto power over the repatriation of even the 1967 displaced persons from Jerusalem, the West Bank and Gaza, not to mention the 30-year diaspora of the Palestinian refugees of 1948 totalling 1.75 million human beings. Mr Begin told President Carter at Camp David that the status and fate of occupied Arab Jerusalem is non-negotiable. The Israeli settlers in Arab Jerusalem and its environs and in the rest of the occupied Arab territories would enjoy extraterritorial rights and privileges, a relic of the age of European colonialism which, everybody is agreed, was a dark and unbridled record of unconscionable domination and exploitation, happily ended by humanity's glorious march towards emancipation in the aftermath of World War II. The Israeli orientation is, perhaps, the unique reversal of this trend and accomplishment which the world vehemently rejects.

Israel has raised a hue and cry over what came to be known as 'linkage', between an Accord on occupied Sinai and an Accord on the other occupied Palestinian and Arab territories. Their objective is unmistakably to divide the Arab world, neutralize Egypt, in order to facilitate their as yet unfinished designs of expansion. How can a viable and lasting peace be accomplished without a comprehensive settlement, the central issue of which is the fate of the Palestinian people? And what are the Israelis so furiously objecting to, and which is presently the subject of discussion at ministerial level at Camp David? Civil autonomy for the remnants of the Palestinian people, to look after the local water and sewage systems, schools and social welfare!

A separate peace with Egypt will be a colossal loss in the long run, and the foremost losers will be none other than the Israelis themselves, because it would, sooner rather than later, aggravate to the breaking point the already explosive situation in the entire region, as it would run counter to the innermost soul of the vast masses of humanity in the Arab and Islamic worlds including, of course, Egypt.

If the Arab–Israeli conflict were an isolated, ephemeral phenomenon and not rooted in the depths of the Arab and Islamic worlds – 800 million people sharing a common legacy of religion, history and civilization, then an American policy-maker, putting aside moral imperatives, may well be tempted to dump the Palestinians as a sad casualty of history and predicate the American national interest and its preservation to their demise.

However, anybody knowledgeable in this huge area with its intense religious affiliation, morals and mores and its common historical experiences in triumphs and adversities over 1,400 years would immediately recognize that such a course of action is nothing less than a recipe for future disaster, out of all proportion to what may appear to be a localized conflict between small feuding nations.[29]

In the aftermath of the declaration pertaining to agreement on concluding a bilateral peace between Egypt and Israel, an extensive review of the situation was carried out concerning the consequences to the Arab World and the international scene and the dimensions of the challenge which confronts the Arab nation in consequence of the conclusion of a separate peace between Israel and Egypt. King Hussein stressed the grave responsibilities which devolve upon the entire Arab nation in confronting the dangers and acting collectively and in close concert to meet them. King Hussein asserted the imperative need to consolidate and augment collective Arab strength, to enable our nation to safeguard and restore its rights. He reiterated that Jordan's position had always been committed to the achievement of a just and comprehensive peace in which all parties participate and the solution of all aspects of the conflict, on the basis of total Israeli withdrawal from all the occupied Arab lands, foremost of which is Holy Jerusalem, and the restoration of all the national rights of the Palestinian people.

King Hussein emphasized the imperative need of mobilizing all components of the Arab nation's capabilities. He also reiterated Jordan's abiding adherence to common Arab action in accordance with the resolutions of the Arab Summit Conference in Baghdad.[32]

The fact that, out of the four front-line States facing Israel, three did not at all, at any stage, participate in the effort, even though they had for one whole decade been doing their utmost to achieve a just, lasting and comprehensive peace, is in itself an eloquent comment on the inadequacy and the fragility of the Camp David arrangement. Nor have the Palestinian people, whether inside the occupied territories or outside them, been consulted or involved in the process, although they are the core of the problem.

Through the years Jordan has steadfastly stood by the three main elements which it considers essential: (a) total withdrawal of Israel from the Arab territories occupied in June 1967; (b) the right to self-determination under conditions of free choice for the Palestinian people, who are at the centre of the Middle East conflict and, of course, their inalienable right to set up their own State and to restore their legitimate rights, their land, and their homes; and (c) the right of all States in the area to live in peace with, if necessary, guarantees of security to all parties.

Jordan's reluctance to join in the peace efforts following Camp David is based not only on its conviction that the peace settlement should be comprehensive and should embrace all aspects of the conflict but also on a careful analysis of Israel's motives and practices in the occupied territories, which Jordan does not find conducive to a just and durable peace.

Any settlements established during a military occupation are in violation of the Fourth Geneva Convention relating to the Protection of Civilian Persons in Time of War. The U.S. Government has in the past consistently and fully supported this position, and has so declared publicly on many occasions. In defiance of international law and practice, and disregarding unanimous world opinion, Israel has continued to establish many more such settlements. It has continued to pursue its policy in this regard, even during the time it was actively engaged in the so-called peace negotiations.

We are seeking to have the international community, represented by its highest executive organ, halt the Israeli practices and policies of establishing these settlements which seriously add to the existing impediments to peace, and to invite a Security Council fact-finding commission to go to the area. That is the least recompense the U.N., which originally brought about the undoing of the Palestinians, owes the Palestinians – to go and see them, to talk to their mayors, to the villagers, to the people whose land and water have been taken over. Let them go into the closed cells of the 30 or so notorious prisons in Israel, and they will find the facts for themselves.[33]

The Ninth Arab Summit which convened in Baghdad (2–5 November 1978) rejected unanimously the Accords negotiated at Camp David. The rejection was made after a most careful scrutiny of the outcome, by Arab Heads of State representing various shades of opinion, because it was felt:

that the Accords prejudice the rights of the Palestinian and Arab peoples in Palestine and the occupied Arab territories; that they had taken place outside the framework of collective Arab responsibility; that they are in contradiction with the Arab Summit Conferences, particularly those held in Algiers and Rabat; that they are in contradiction with the charter of the Arab League and the relevant resolutions of the U.N. pertaining to the question of Palestine, and would not, therefore, lead to the just peace which the Arab nation aspires to.

The Arab Summit, therefore, decides to disapprove the two Accords and to disassociate itself from them and to reject any political, economic, legal and other consequences which may devolve upon them.

What the Ninth Arab Summit rejected was not peace but an unjust peace. The U.N. itself would have acted likewise in the light of its Charter and its own resolutions on the conflict. A just peace must specify two basic elements: (a) withdrawal from all the territories occupied in 1967, foremost of which is Arab Jerusalem; (b) the restoration of the legitimate rights of the Palestinian people, as recognized by the U.N. resolutions and the dictates of natural justice.[26]

18 Arab States and the P.L.O. at the Baghdad Arab Summit held in the month of March 1979 turned down the Accords as not being conducive to a just and comprehensive peace but, on the contrary, an impediment to its achievement. Hitherto, the Arab states had been categorized either as rejectionists or as moderates. For the first time they found themselves in unanimity, overcoming ideological, geographical and all other considerations.[34]

During the third week of November 1979, 21 Arab States and the P.L.O. participated in the Tenth Arab Summit Conference and issued the final Declaration reiterating that the Palestinian question is at the core of the long-drawn-out struggle in which the Arabs are engaged against Zionism and all the dangers that Zionism poses militarily, politically, economically and culturally, and which threaten the fate of the Arab nation in its entirety.

The recent Arab Summit Conference did not in any way slam the door on a just peace. To the contrary, it said:

The Summit asserts that the Arab nation is struggling to achieve a just peace, based on principles of right and justice and the restoration of the inalienable national rights of the Palestinian people and the liberation of all the occupied Palestinian and Arab lands.

The Arab nation is resolved to meet the challenge and to struggle for the restoration of its usurped rights and to build a future where peace and justice prevail. It fully appreciates that the struggle against Zionism is a fateful struggle, a struggle for civilization which requires that it be guided by the values of the Arab nation and the consecration of all its solidarity, common purpose and resolve.

The kings and presidents of the Arab World have reiterated in the Declaration their condemnation of the Camp David Accords and the Egyptian–Israeli peace treaty and their unequivocal rejection of them and all the consequences that would flow therefrom.

They also assert their support to the struggle of the Palestine Arab people, under the leadership of the P.L.O., their sole legitimate representative.[46]

What went wrong to make the Accords so unpalatable to so many throughout the Arab and Islamic worlds and the third world, and a muted expression of intense scepticism in much of the rest of the world?

The main reason is that the Accords basically altered the premises upon which a just and lasting peace could be achieved. It literally turned the tables upside down. It circumvented the major assumptions pertaining to the restoration of the legitimate rights of the Palestinian people in their homeland and the universally recognized principles of international law and equity on the inadmissibility of the acquisition of territory by force.

The Accords in effect (and intentions notwithstanding) legalize Israeli occupation in perpetuity, even though masquerading under the spurious term 'relocation of forces', on equally spurious security grounds.

For the uninitiated in the sordid and tragic conflict in the Middle East, the home-rule or autonomy plan enshrined in the Accords seems ostensibly an improvement over the present status of outright military occupation. Its ultimate effect, however, would be to neutralize and disenfranchise the 1.2 million Palestinians who are still living within the occupied territories, while retaining the territories themselves as an Israeli domain. It is an ingenious solution, therefore, to an Israeli dilemma which relishes the territories while rejecting the indigenous Palestinian people who live on them.[34]

Israel would have annexed all the territories but for the fact that the Israelis do not wish to enfranchise the 1.2 million Palestinians in addition to 600,000 so-called Israeli Palestinian Arabs, because that would upset the racial purity and exclusiveness of the Israeli State.

The self-rule plan therefore is intended to gain time in order that the existing population pass away by natural attrition and inevitable death or, if this does not work efficiently enough, they will be strangulated by sequestrating whatever has remained of the land, water and other resources without which they will not be able to survive.[40]

If anyone thinks that the home-rule concept represents an original or novel contribution by the Camp David Accords, then all he has to do is to consult with the leaders and mayors of the occupied West Bank and the Gaza Strip. They will recall that the plan had been floated and discussed with them by Mr Shimon Peres, as far back as 1974 when he was Minister of Defence. They had unanimously rejected his plan as offering practically no improvement on their plight under occupation.

The autonomy proposals which I outlined do not encompass the Arab sector of Jerusalem and its environs. For Israel had annexed Arab Jerusalem, a city hallowed by two billion adherents of the Christian and Islamic faiths; that annexation alone, and its perpetuation, would torpedo any and all efforts towards a peaceful resolution of the conflict and would eventually trigger conflict in which far more than the Arab World would inevitably be involved. To the Islamic World, Jerusalem is the first Qibla to which people turned their faces for prayer. Israeli claims to exclusivity on national or religious grounds would impinge upon the national rights of the Palestinians.

Speaking before the Knesset on 20 March 1979, the Prime Minister of Israel stated: 'Israel will never return to the pre-1967 lines.' Replying to the Prime Minister of Egypt on Jerusalem, Mr Begin said: 'Mark my words, united Jerusalem is the eternal capital of Israel.' He declared that in what he termed Judea, Samaria and Gaza, 'there will never be a Palestinian State'. As for Palestinian self-rule, he said: 'We never agreed to autonomy for the territories but for the inhabitants.'

The Labour Party opposition leader, Mr Peres, took exception to Begin's autonomy. He said: 'Realistically, I cannot see how you can separate self-government from a territory. Can you really distinguish between a man and his house, a farmer and his field? It is impossible!'

Under the Accords, Jordan has been placed in an impossible position and assigned a role which can only be described as degrading and unthinkable. The Jordan Government, which is basically constrained after the Rabat Summit Conference (when responsibility for the occupied sector of Jerusalem and the West Bank devolved upon the P.L.O. together with the overall Palestine question), has been assigned by the Accords the role of one of four policemen, under Israeli occupation, during the transition period of five years. Compounding the situation is the fact that, after the transition period, one would not see the end of the tunnel. We are told that in the long run things will work themselves out; but in the long run we will all be dead.[34]

Jordan's commitment to a just and lasting peace has been consistent and persevering. No one in the know would contest this fact. Why then has Jordan, in concert with the rest of the Arab World, baulked at the current peace efforts, pursued outside the auspices of the U.N.? The answer is clear-cut and overwhelming. Jordan has found itself with no alternative but to reject the Camp David Accords because of very substantive and inescapable considerations. The reasons are manifold but can be summed up as follows:

(1) The framework prescribed for a solution to the occupied territories, foremost of which is Jerusalem, is *a priori* flawed, inasmuch as it specifically tolerates a perpetuation of military occupation indefinitely.

The provision in the Camp David Accords about relocation of Israeli troops to specified areas within the occupied territories is no more than a military and, perhaps, political convenience. It does not end military occupation. You can walk the streets of New York, London or Paris and come across hardly a single soldier. Does this mean that there are no military forces in those three great countries to defend their realms? Certainly there are, but they are stationed where they should be, to defend their own country and citizenry. Israeli military relocation, on the other hand, can only be intended to perpetuate the subjugation of the occupied people, like Big Brother watching over the good behaviour of his subdued subjects.

And if reasons of security are advanced, we should emphatically point out that the weak are invariably more in need of security than the strong.

Furthermore, the prospects of a lasting peace can never be balanced upon the sharp edge of the bayonet.

(2) Jordan vehemently rejects any proposition which would reduce its proud and closest kin and partners to the status of tutelage under Israeli overlordship. It is an insult to human dignity and an affront to an indomitable people. Their provisional sovereign independence over Palestine had been recognized by the League of Nations almost 70 years ago, and now, when decolonization has all but been accomplished, we are being asked to acquiesce in their diminution to a so-called self-rule, over disparate and dismembered reservations, bereft of any of the meaningful attributes of freedom, geographic cohesion, self-determination and independence, present or future.

(3) Oblivious to repeated U.N. resolutions and the accepted norms of human rights, the displaced, the dispossessed and the refugees shall remain in exile in perpetuity, save for a tiny few who may be repatriated at the selective pleasure of the occupation and subject to their veto. And even under such circumscribed conditions, the returnees, by the end of the five-year transition, will find hardly any land which they can settle on, if the Israelis persist – as they insist they will – in their self-proclaimed policy and practice of relentless sequestration, colonization and annexation. In short, the Palestinians, the lawful owners of the land, have been treated as objects and impediments to be dispensed with, in due course, and not as free and lawful citizens of their own ancestral homeland.[45]

Successful diplomacy is essentially the working out of a viable *modus vivendi* between two disputing parties, with which both sides can live, if it is to endure. The fixation upon one outcome which has been the case in the Camp David Accords and resorting to arm-twisting, psychological warfare and other forms of pressure can only be counter-productive and inimical to the best interests of the U.S.A., throughout the region, already exacerbated by an accumulated record of lavish partiality to one side and self-righteous arrogance in dealing with the other sides.

If my readings of current thinking here are correct, the present trend, after the Accords, seems to be to revert to gunboat diplomacy, long outdated and repudiated, particularly after Vietnam.

Besides, legitimate and vital business can never be conducted in regions afflicted by turmoil. This need not be the case if the vast masses of the region are dealt with as potential or actual friends and not as potential adversaries. If this persists, it may well become a self-fulfilling prophecy, with disastrous consequences to all.

There are two scenarios and approaches which I wish to present as alternatives to the Camp David Accords.

First, if Israel is unwilling to entertain a partition of Palestine – as were the Palestinians in 1947 – then the Israelis and the Palestinians will find themselves in a convergence of views rather than a divergence. There is only one condition that the Palestinians will insist upon, namely the right of return of all Palestinian refugees and displaced except, of course, those who may not wish to exercise this inalienable option and opt for compensation.

A unified bi-national or federal State or States can then be worked out in direct talks between the Government of Israel and the legitimate representatives of the Palestinian people, the P.L.O., or whomever they designate, on the constitutional niceties, of restructuring such a State or States. Representation would be on the basis of universal suffrage. This would not be a dismantling of Israel, as the Israeli apologists claim. It would simply be a final solution of the Palestine problem in one stroke; a termination of the tragic and explosive ordeal of the refugees; and not least a termination, once and for all, of all belligerency, conflict, back-breaking military expenditures, and the equally devastating malaise of living in anxiety, fear, hatred and all the other ills which prolonged conflicts inevitably generate. A new period of friendship, cooperation and undreamed-of prosperity would be ushered in, and its blessings would encompass not only the Israelis and Palestinians but the whole region and beyond, the world at large.

The financial ramifications of such a solution are well within the capabilities of the region, including the Palestinians, as well as interim assistance from the outside, in a cause which may well, in the final analysis, spell the difference between war and peace. The U.S.A. was enriched, not impoverished, by its open-door policy; it would be extremely awkward if the Israelis were to continue predicating their policy on counting how many Palestinians there are, or how many new-born babies or deaths. This is negative, self-tormenting and futile. It is based on fear, not on hope. The Palestinians should have been in their homeland as of right in the first place. And even the 1947 partition plan did not envisage their dispersal either from the proposed Jewish State or, of course, from the Palestinian Arab State. What I am proposing, therefore, lays no claims to originality; it is simply a resuscitation of what should have been all along. An important and additional bonus to this sweeping approach is that it would automatically solve war-torn Lebanon's ordeal and enable it, overnight, to begin the arduous task of reconstruction and rehabilitation. There need then be no U.N. forces in the region, and it is perfectly feasible, if Israel and the P.L.O. agree, to arrange a suspension of all warlike activities during the interim period of negotiations. If successful, such activities become totally redundant. The U.N. would breathe a sigh of relief when, after 30 years, it would be asked to delete the scores of items on Palestine and the Middle East from its agenda.

The alternative to this first approach would be an exclusive, theocratic approach, at an escalating exorbitant price which the world can ill afford. If Israel prefers partition, then the solution would be along the lines of Security Council resolution 242 and other related resolutions on the rights of the refugees. This means withdrawal from the Arab sector of Jerusalem, the West Bank and the Gaza Strip, as well as rescinding the substantial colonization already made on Palestinian territory. The details could be worked out.

It would become the national homeland of the Palestinians and their State (most likely in federation or some similar link with Jordan) and Jordanians and Palestinians alike would freely decide the form of linkage and self-determination. Every Palestinian who wishes to belong there should be unconditionally entitled to do so.

Although a solution along those lines is acceptable to the Palestinian people, as well as to the Arab World, as emerged at the Baghdad Arab Summit, it is my personal view – and I am not thinking at this point either as Ambassador of Jordan or on behalf of the Palestinians – that it would leave some residues of the sordid old-time conflict. Both sides would start bickering over security or presumed security which can translate into such provisions as the relocation of forces (which, in fact, is an excuse for additional acquisition of the substantially shrunken Palestinian territory). It would require a prolonged U.N. presence. It would leave numerous Palestinian refugees unredeemed and a sizeable number of Israeli zealots uneasy, in consequence of a divided territory. It would retain the psychological consciousness of the 'we' and the 'you', thus inhibiting, though not thwarting, mutuality of interests.

Again thinking as an individual, I believe the first scenario would be more lasting and inherently self-perpetuating. It is up to the official leaderships of the two peoples to determine which would be the better approach, or if some combination of the two can be formed. Jordan, Syria and the Lebanon would have an important say, since the outcome impinges directly on them.

As I look ahead over the next decade or two, I cannot but read two signals and see two scenarios. First, a Middle East in harmony, peace and breath-taking development and prosperity, literally a golden age of creativity. Alternatively, a scenario too gruesome even to contemplate. The world will not survive its second millennium A.D. There will be an atomic conflict; this is Armageddon.

Looking ahead over the next decade or two, and if the Palestine and Middle East questions are not resolved, it is incredible how close to reality fantasies can turn out to be.

Let us not be suicidal, fatalistic and self-destructive. Let us hope and pray that the first scenario of everlasting peace, justice and prosperity can be made to prevail.[34]

14
Zionism, Hegemonism and Nuclearization

Zionism

Are the Israelis above the law?

Is the world divided into an omnipotent race and subservient Gentiles born into this world to serve the aims of the master race? We, the Gentiles, are several billion human souls, and yet how much weight, I wonder, do we carry in the councils of some of the mighty.

Time Magazine published a revealing story that, every day, a Mr Rothschild meets with a cabal in London behind closed doors, to fix the price of gold. A telex is sent out to agents around the world to observe the price. This, of course, extends to monetary and other financial manipulations. How can the billions of struggling humanity compete with such awesome power, except by their indomitable spirit and their unshakeable faith in justice, equality, goodness and the inherent worth of the individual?

If anyone should doubt the truth of my statement, let us take a cursory look at the Israelis' sordid record – and the list is just the tip of the iceberg. In the mid-1940s, Lord Moyne, Minister of State and member of the British War Cabinet, was murdered in Cairo, because the Zionist movement did not feel comfortable with his views. He was in charge of the British war effort in the entire Middle East. Towards the end of the 1940s, one of the most patriotic and dedicated American statesmen, the first American Secretary of Defense, was dismissed and subjected to such ruthless harassment for almost six months that he committed suicide. Of course, Mr Truman who dismissed him became President of the U.S.A.

Count Bernadotte, the U.N. mediator, was shot dead in the streets of Jerusalem because the Israelis did not like his views on the peaceful settlement of the conflict.

Mr William Rogers, a man of great integrity and patriotism, was dismissed from his office of Secretary of State, because he dared present a solution to the Arab–Israeli conflict, based on the provisions of Security Council resolution 242 and a repatriation of substantial numbers of Palestinian refugees.

In 1967 the U.S. Sixth Fleet was prevented from coming to the rescue of one of its beleaguered and ruthlessly attacked ships for nine hours by the Israeli air and naval forces, resulting in numerous casualties to American citizens, let alone the prestige of the U.S.A. One of the two Rostrow brothers ('ardent Zionists') prevailed on the late President Johnson not to take any action, on political grounds.

Governor Scranton, former Permanent Representative of the U.S.A. to the U.N., after a return from a Middle East trip committed the unforgivable sin of suggesting that U.S. policy towards the Middle East should be 'even-handed'. These two words cost him his political career.[32]

It was in the second part of the nineteenth century that the European Jews, emboldened by their growing financial, commercial and political power, tempted by the accelerating weakness of the Ottoman Empire and dejected by growing anti-Semitism in Europe, partly in reaction to their increasing power, intrigues and refusal to assimilate within the societies in which they lived, began their dreams, plans and activities to seize Palestine, long before Herzel wrote his book entitled *The Jewish State*. People like Bernbaum, Nordau, Klatzkin and others were atheists, but propagated Zionism as an ethnic and nationalist ideology.

In the latter part of the nineteenth century, an emissary representing the Rothschilds and other Jewish banking houses approached the High Porte at Istanbul with an offer to pay off the Ottoman Empire's huge debts in exchange for giving Palestine to the Jews as a homeland. Sultan Abdul Hamid, pretending ignorance, asked: 'What towns and cities does Palestine comprise?' The emissary began citing the names of Jaffa, Haifa, Acre, Gaza, etc., until he mentioned Jerusalem. At that point Abdul Hamid angrily interrupted his visitor and told him: 'Jerusalem – Qudus Shareef! Why don't we make the bargain over Istanbul, but not Jerusalem?' From then on the Jews never ceased their intrigues against the Empire, including false and nominal conversions of Turkish Jews to Islam to undermine the Empire from within. It was they who worked at undermining Islam in the name of Tauranian nationalism, who instigated the persecution of the Arabs and led to the great Arab Rebellion which expressed not only the Arab cultural heritage, but also dismay at the Ottoman Government's increasing deviation from the brotherhood of Islam.

The Zionist movement first turned to Germany and to France for assistance in usurping Palestine. But since its leaders saw in Britain a more responsive ally and since Britain, a sprawling empire, would be the horse to back, they used it as the focal point of their activities. They succeeded in obtaining the Balfour Declaration in 1917.

Needless to repeat that the said Declaration has no legal validity whatsoever. It was simply the outcome of a confluence of interests between a colonial power needing a vassal to safeguard its lines of communications in the Middle East, Asia and Australia, and a Zionist leadership which interpreted Jewishness not in terms of religion, but in terms of race, country and a dogged refusal to assimilate with others.

Even the inclusion of the Balfour Declaration in the mandates awarded by the League of Nations was an illegitimate aggression against the lawful inhabitants of Palestine, and in face of their vehement opposition.

The truth is that anyone who has carefully read the history of the emergence of Zionism, including the memoirs of the Zionist leaders themselves, could not fail to realize that it was motivated by the following:

(1) The ethnic, racial and nationalistic consciousness of a handful of Jewish thinkers and fanatics.

(2) Most of those leaders were atheist, or at least did not adhere to Judaism as a religion, but as a nationalism.

(3) They acknowledged the inability of the Jewish communities to integrate with the societies in which they had lived.

(4) The foremost supporters of Zionism were simultaneously the most vehement anti-Semites. This applied to Lloyd George and

Balfour himself. The pro-Zionist anti-Semites wanted to get rid of the Jews living within their midst at any cost, and they proposed such countries as Kenya, Uganda and even Iraq as the promised homeland.

(5) The Zionist founders and leaders were always ready to play the role of agent and satellite for whichever power was willing to support their cause.

(6) The majority of the Jewish communities of those days, including those in the U.S.A., were against Zionism because they feared that, if successful, it would create 'dual loyalties' which would endanger their status in the countries in which they lived and prospered. But as the early Zionist leaders rightly predicted, animosity among the Jews towards Zionism would disappear once the Zionists achieved their goals. Success brings more success and the Jews opposed to Zionism today are an insignificant minority throughout the world.

(7) Once the Zionist venture had been launched, falsely in the name of religion, the masses of Jews found themselves in a position where they must either expand and grow stronger against their adversaries or face the prospect of being vanquished themselves, in a sea of hostility created against the Jews by Zionism itself. It is not surprising therefore that they foment anti-Semitism wherever they can, to augment their numbers.[35]

Within the universal context of recognition of the imperative to eliminate *all forms* of racial discrimination, the General Assembly on 10 November 1975 adopted resolution 3379, equating racism with Zionism. It interpreted a situation as it really was and still is, and had the moral integrity and courage to say so loudly and clearly. Israel and several of its supporters raised a tremendous hue and cry which reverberated and almost wrecked the various organs of the U.N. Why? I suppose, because it is unpleasant to look hypo-critical, inconsistent or insincere. How can anybody who is true to himself or to humanity's values and ideals fail to see that uprooting a people, human beings like ourselves, is a form of racial discrimi-nation in its ultimate form? A Palestinian either in the diaspora or in captivity is discriminated against, not because he is good or bad; he is unabashedly discriminated against for the sole sin of being a Palestinian and not belonging to the Jewish race or faith. It is as simple as that: he is punished because of the accident of his birth, his race and his spiritual affiliation.

We have nothing against Judaism as a religion, or against the Jews as people. On the contrary, we share with it a wide spectrum of religious experiences. But one's freedom becomes licence, exclusiveness and privilege when it results in the destruction of the lives and freedom of others. Is this not what laws, human or divine, prescribe? If we allow ourselves to compromise universally accepted principles, then we will have betrayed and possibly wrecked all the values and the rationale for the existence of the U.N. If we bend to accommodate the strong or the privileged for any reason whatsoever, then it won't be long before we find that we have reverted to the laws of the jungle and leave behind all the talk about fundamental human rights. Justice, as Plato stressed, is the central goal of any workable society, and so it should be with international communities.

The ultimate form of racial discrimination is not merely the denial of self-determination on grounds of prejudice and avarice; it is the denial of a people's birthright over their soil and the right to determine their own fate. This is precisely what the Israeli Zionists openly proclaim and practise in Palestine.[21]

The Zionists have indeed gone a long way towards achieving this goal both in terms of land and in terms of population. There should be no mistake about it. There can be no solution to the Arab–Israeli conflict so long as Israel continues to be dominated by Zionist nationalism, which is the antithesis of the true Judaic ancient spiritual relationship to parts of the Holy Land – a relationship that we recognize. Indeed, the truly religious regard the establishment of Israel in the mundane sense as sacrilegious and categorically refuse to recognize it or even to deal with it.

In 1951, a rabbi at Princeton said to me, 'I agree with everything you have said but, believe me, we have been threatened that unless we toe the line we will not be buried in Jewish cemeteries.'

In 1919, before the Zionists gained a stranglehold on American Jews, by means fair and foul, a memorandum signed by 300 prominent American Jews was presented to the Peace Conference through President Wilson. Those distinguished American Jews stated:

We raise our voices, in warning and protest, against the demand of the Zionists for the reorganization of the Jews as a national unit, to whom now or in the future, territorial sovereignty in Palestine shall be committed... The re-establishment in Palestine of a distinctively Jewish State is utterly opposed to the principles of democracy which it is the avowed purpose of the World Peace Conference to establish... To unite church and State, in any form, as under the old Jewish Hierarchy, would be a leap backward of two thousand years... We ask that Palestine be constituted as a free and independent State, to be governed under a democratic form of government, recognizing no distinctions of creed or race or ethnic descent, and with adequate power to protect the country against oppression of any kind. We do not wish to see Palestine, either now or at any time in the future, organized as [an exclusively] Jewish State.

Professor Morris Jastrow, one of those who signed that memorandum, wrote in *Zionism and the Future of Palestine*:

I should like to envisage a Palestine that may become a beacon-light for the world, that may again become a spiritual focus, furnishing further inspiration for mankind... Such a Palestine, however, cannot be built up through the creation of a Jewish State. A Jewish State would simply mean a glorified ghetto, narrow in its outlook, undemocratic in its organization, and that may well turn out to be reactionary in its tendencies.

We have seen how progressive it has turned out to be.

The Neturei Karta of the U.S.A., a Jewish religious organization, has published declarations on many occasions since 1947 opposing a Jewish State in Palestine. One of the latest declarations was a letter to the Secretary-General of the U.N., Mr Kurt Waldheim, published in the *Wall Street Journal* of 13 November 1975, which states: 'We would like to call to your attention that even after 27 years of the State of Israel's existence, there are large numbers of Jews in the Holy Land and in the entire world who are opposed to Zionists and to the Zionist State...' But we know that any dissenting voice is immediately silenced and its owner even accused of treason. 'The Zionist State has usurped without justification the holy name of Israel. Torah-true Jews wish to live in peace and harmony with their neighbours and with the community of nations.'

Thus, there might have been a totally different, more humane, more civilized and more tranquil turn of events in the whole of the Middle East region if the original handful of zealots, helped enormously by the inhumanity of other peoples, let alone imperialist designs in other regions of the world, had not inflicted their views upon the masses of ordinary Jews in Europe. But why should that have been taken out on the Palestinians who in those days did not even know of what was happening elsewhere. That was in the days before the radio and television, and communciations were extremely poor.[52]

It is hardly recognized, at least publicly, that the Zionist enterprise of endless aggression is directly and indirectly responsible for the serious economic ills which afflict the economies of the world – both developed and developing – directly and indirectly, in a chain reaction which started with the closure of the Suez Canal in 1967, the Israeli refusal to withdraw from the occupied territories, to the 1973 war and its economic consequences, and the end is by no means in sight. The tens of millions of unemployed, the stunted growth of the developing world, the disastrous inflation which has deeply affected the lives of hundreds of millions of people are but a part of the price which the world is paying, in consequence of insatiable Zionist expansion.[54]

Hegemonism

It is almost tautological to attempt a definition of the term hegemony. Even though the concept is an old one, it seems to have re-emerged in the debates of our world body in recent years. In essence, it means the strivings by States or groups of States to place under subjugation, to exercise (by covert or overt action) undue and illegitimate, overriding influence over the behaviour and decision-making process of other States and peoples. It could take the form of imperialism, the continual physical expansion and annexation of other States and peoples. Concomitant to imperialism was the phenomenon of colonialism, likewise the occupation of other States and peoples' territories and the exploitation of their sweat and their natural resources.

The final Declaration of the Conference of Heads of State or Government of Non-aligned Countries which met in Havana in September 1979 contained the following excerpt:

National independence, sovereignty and territorial integrity, sovereign equality and the free social development of all countries; independence of non-aligned countries from great-power or bloc rivalries and influences and opposition to participation in military pacts and alliances arising therefrom; the struggle against imperialism, colonialism, neo-colonialism, racism, including Zionism and all forms of expansionism, foreign occupation and domination and hegemony; active peaceful coexistence among all States; non-interference and non-intervention in the internal and external affairs of other countries; freedom of all States to determine their political systems and pursue economic, social and cultural development without intimidation, hindrance and pressure; establishment of a new international economic order and development of international cooperation on the basis of equality; the right to self-determination and independence of all peoples under colonial and alien domination and constant support to the struggle of national liberation movements; respect for human rights and fundamental freedoms; opposition to the division of the world into antagonistic military-political alliances and blocs and rejection of outmoded doctrines such as spheres of influence and balance of terror; permanent sovereignty over natural resources; inviolability of legally established international boundaries; non-use of force, or threat of use of force and non-recognition of situations brought about by the threat or use of force; and peaceful settlements of disputes.

Even the voluminous Oxford Dictionary could not have spelt out in greater detail what the term hegemony really means. And yet, the 95 States of the non-aligned found it imperative to give such a detailed description. I need hardly state that it was not as an exercise in semantics that they found it necessary to do so. For it was a sincere and profound reflection upon the state of affairs and the state of mind which evidently have relapsed into acquiescence, acceptance and even the declared advocacy of the policy of hegemonism and the old game of nations and power politics, in conducting international relations.

We had all been under the impression that the U.N. Charter had irretrievably replaced the abominable policies of expansion, occupation and hegemony. We had been witnessing, over the past 25 years, the glorious process of decolonization, and have always regarded its almost total achievement as a hallmark in the annals of the U.N. We have been bracing ourselves to a process no less important in magnitude than the striving to achieve a more viable and equitable new international economic order.

And yet, as we scan the panorama of world politics, we are witnessing the frightening spectre of a retrogression into the ways of the nineteenth and the early twentieth century, when imperialism, colonialism, exploitation and hegemony were not only recognized norms of behaviour, but were even a source of unbridled boasting and pride: the scramble for Africa and elsewhere; such anachronistic doctrines as 'the white man's burden' and the 'manifest destiny'; the civilizing missions which not only dismally failed to civilize anyone but merely brutalized man's vision of the world and his relationships with his fellow beings. It climaxed into two savage World Wars in which untold millions perished and those who had survived suffered immeasurably.

History is an indispensable teacher for any statesman, but so is an incisive comprehension of the frailties of human nature: Metternich's power game, Bismarck's grandiose plans or Hitler's outright bid for racist hegemony were not only disastrous but were perpetrated within the survival confines of the military capabilities which prevailed in the nineteenth and early twentieth century.

Surely, present-day policy-makers must necessarily be reminded that the world is approaching the end of the twentieth century. The stark fact is that there is a difference in kind and not in degree, in consequence of technological developments, which have for the first time in man's recorded history given him the capability of destroying himself and the world. A new chapter has been written which must remain in our consciousness and subdue even our subconscious instincts.

The world can no longer afford to play the unconscionable game of nations. As His Holiness Pope Paul II, speaking on disarmament at the General Assembly recently, warned: one day, someone, sometime, somewhere will be tempted to unleash the vast accumulation of nuclear and other weaponry to destroy the world.

Mr Litvinov, the Foreign Minister of the Soviet Union in the 1930s, gave repeated warnings at the League of Nations against the dangers of policies of hegemonism. He was unheeded, and World War II was the consequence.

Indeed, President Woodrow Wilson in the aftermath of World

War I had preached, but to no avail, the humane 14 points, the same points which are presently the foundation-stone of non-alignment, including the right of every people to self-determination.

We all realize that human nature, with its gregarious as well as its pugnacious instincts, cannot be easily altered or transformed. And yet it must, considering that the world is literally, not metaphorically, living in the shadow of impending death. Any crisis, anywhere, in a world of interdependence can, by accident or faulty miscalculation, ignite a terminal conflagration.

It is for this reason, let alone all the moral foundations of what should be a friendly and equitable world order, that there must be a transmutation of consciousness on the part of all of us. We can either survive by scrupulously abiding by the rule of both law and morality or perish by the unprecedented sharp edge of the sword in the nuclear age.

Concerns for security are legitimate and understandable. Competing ideological systems aimed at influencing others are also understandable. But any nation can influence other nations far more by friendly and cooperative behaviour than by the diplomacy of the gun and the concept of war as an extension of diplomacy.

It is my earnest hope that the policy-makers in the world, and particularly the major powers, will not scoff at what they might regard as naive preaching. . . but even if they do, it is the only salvation of a turbulent world.[41]

Nuclearization

The General Assembly held a historic special session between 23 May and 30 June 1978 which was tantamount to ringing the alarm bell by almost all Member States over the survival and fate of the world, in consequence of the acceleration and proliferation of the monstrous and terminal nuclear arsenals.

World opinion and articulate and concerned organizations, all the world over, watched the proceedings with a mixture of apprehension, hope and guarded expectation that the historic session might be a turning point, a heightened dimension of awareness, if not a hallmark in arresting, stabilizing and eventually achieving the deeply cherished goal of complete and total disarmament. It is in this spirit that Jordan warmly welcomed the Salt II Agreement between the U.S.A. and the U.S.S.R., not as the be-all and end-all but as a first step towards complete and total disarmament for the salvation of our planet, our only habitable planet.

We are likewise irrevocably convinced that unless practical and effective measures are taken to deal with the most ominous issue of Israeli nuclear armament, it may very well someday, somehow bring about a nuclear holocaust, not only to the region of the Middle East and beyond, but to the world in its entirety. Whether Israel is maintaining a threshold capability or has indeed chosen the nuclear option and has already acquired its own arsenal, as a means of achieving its political and strategic objectives, is not the crux of the matter, even though almost all knowledgeable people are thoroughly convinced, on the basis of credible evidence, that the monster has for some years been let out of Israel's Pandora's box.

What is the crux of the matter is that as far back as 1950, and this was a mental and psychological decision of intent, the Israeli leadership determined to pursue the nuclear option, in pursuit of a carefully laid-down policy of territorial expansion, political blackmail and hegemony in its various manifestations. The late Mr Ben Gurion decreed the establishment of an Atomic Energy Commission in 1950, accountable directly to himself as Prime Minister, with the avowed purpose of assiduously working towards the acquisition of nuclear know-how.

The decision, however, seemed to have very little impact, if any, on the international community, still under the misguided spell of a helpless Israel surrounded by enemies bent upon destroying it, even though a mere two years earlier it was the Palestinian people whose national existence had been destroyed in their homeland and the majority of them uprooted.

Israeli nuclear activities continued unabated under the very eyes of the major powers whose data gathering no one should underrate. Indeed, some of the most prominent scientists in this very field, whose emotional commitments to Israel were highly pronounced, were generously given visas to visit Israel, ostensibly to attend scientific conferences, but without due regard being given to the potential implications of such visits in the form of transfer of nuclear know-how, while at the same time other American scientists with different national derivations, including Arab and particularly Palestinian scientists who had attained excellence in the U.S.A., were denied even social visits to their next-of-kin and were placed under strict surveillance, notwithstanding the fact that many of their countries of origin did not possess either the installations or the intention to engage in this dangerous game.

In the meantime, and in a spurt of anger the reckless French Government in the pre-de Gaulle era, angered by the Arab World's support for Algeria's war of liberation, provided Israel with the Dimona nuclear reactor, big enough to possess the capability of upgrading its uranium fuel into plutonium weaponry capability, as well as the required scientists to enhance its acquisition.

In 1964 Jordan received irrefutable evidence that Israel had achieved the threshold of nuclear capability and that it required a little while longer to perfect its delivery system. As I came to that year's session I took the opportunity to raise the matter with the then distinguished Secretary of State, Mr Dean Rusk, who apparently did not seem wholly in the picture. When I gave him the evidence which we had somehow obtained, emanating from an atomic scientist-engineer who had been working in both Dimona and a French reactor in the outskirts of Paris, Mr Rusk agreed to my request for an investigation, while conceding the considerable difficulties that would be encountered in such a search. Two months later, the U.S. Ambassador in Amman informed me that the U.S.A. had been able to establish the accuracy of my Government's reports. He added that the U.S.A., with all the difficulties encountered, had been surprised by its own findings as to the magnitude of Israel's nuclear achievement.

What I have said so far is but a genesis of what I regard as the 'original sin'. The net result has been that Israel has become the sixth or seventh nuclearized country in the world.

The Israeli case as far as the U.S.A. is concerned, which clearly runs counter to the U.S.A.'s best interests, is seemingly compromised by the special U.S.–Israel relationship, essentially anchored in the U.S.A.'s political imperatives. The U.S.A. seems incapable of unilaterally acting to deprive the Israelis of their announced nuclear capability, by threatening to cut off its huge financial, economic, military and political support.

The Israelis themselves have made what could only be construed as a public disclosure. Their former President, a scientist himself, made such a disclosure in a television statement which many people in Amman heard. The stealing of fissionable material from U.S. atomic installations and the piracy in the open seas, some two years ago, of 200 tons of enriched uranium leave no room for doubt whither Israel has gone and is continuing to go.

In 1968, the former U.S. Secretary of State, Mr Dean Rusk, declared:

> The spread of nuclear weapons would aggravate our difficulties in maintaining friendly relations with parties to a continuing dispute. If one party 'went nuclear', we might have to decide whether to help the other party, directly or through security assurances, whether to sever economic aid to the country acquiring atomic weapons, or whether to stand aside, even though the result might be a war which would be hard to contain.

How true and rational his analysis was and yet, despite devastating evidence that Israel was actually reprocessing the fissionable material for weaponry use (which could not have escaped the highly sophisticated detection of America's arms control apparatus) no measures have been taken to end Israel's nuclearization.

Indeed, in 1970 the head of the Egyptian atomic installation in Egypt, a top-level atomic scientist, briefed us on Israeli nuclear activity and mentioned the construction by Israel of a high tower to dispose of dangerous waste as one of the many proofs that Israel had been engaged in the production process. He even calculated how much production was being made per annum.

I need hardly elaborate on further evidence of Israel's nuclearization because facts have become too abundant to leave any room for doubt. The political and strategic implications of the dangerous development, namely the transformation from the 'prenuclear' situation to the 'postnuclear', compellingly confronts us with an unacceptable situation, for which no clear-cut, fully-thought-out doctrine for action has been formulated or is in existence, by the superpowers.

The fact that Israel has not declared itself unequivocally as having transformed itself deliberately and by calculation does not in any way belittle the overall implications to the stability, security and even survival of hundreds of millions of people in the region; Israel holding nuclear weapons of devastation poised will sooner or later compel political and strategic decisions contrary to the peace, stability and survival of the world. It is the more impelling and dangerous when judged against Israel's openly declared expansion-

ist policies and its adamant refusal to agree on a fair and just
solution to the conflict of the Middle East and the redemption of
the Palestinian people. Quite apart from the Israeli leadership's
intransigence, our people are convinced that the acquisition of an
atomic arsenal has been an overriding factor in Israel's disregard of
all precepts of international law, basic norms of justice, and the
international will of the U.N., as categorically embodied in its
numerous decisions.

It is perfectly true that the late President Lyndon Johnson stressed to Prime Minister Eshkol as early as 1964 'that the U.S.A. was
against proliferation of nuclear weapons in the world and she was
certainly against their proliferation in the Middle East'. But those
grave warnings have never been translated into effective measures
to forestall proliferation.

I can well understand pampering a favoured child. But what no
one seemingly can understand is that when you do pamper a child,
you give him a reasonably harmless toy, not a pistol so that, by
accident, design or the child growing up in an unhealthy atmos-
phere, he is given the wherewithal to kill and turn into an international monster. If I had such a child, I would regard him as a
danger to the family – in this case, to the family of nations.

The Israelis are presently committed to preserving the post-1967
status quo, which means a total national obliteration of the Palestinian people on their homeland. The temptation might extend to
attempting the creation of more and more *status quos* by Israeli
atomic blackmail. Quite clearly, the already victimized and the
newly threatened by atomic blackmail will not in the long run
accept their own demise with folded arms. There could then arise a
variety of scenarios, each of which portends grave dangers to world
peace and security. To begin with, a nuclear capability does not
and will not preclude legitimate resistance to occupation and the
restoration of Palestinian Arab rights, atom bombs or no atom
bombs.

Secondly, the whole concept of non-proliferation loses its moral
as well as its practical efficacy when proliferation is acquiesced in,
not necessarily by design but by inaction. Future generations will
not tolerate a situation of atomic blackmail placing them in a situation of perpetual bondage. If my reading of human nature is correct, the victimized and threatened will try to break loose, thus
dealing a fatal blow to the doctrine of non-proliferation which is

presently one of the pillars of international security in the nuclear age.

The resolutions which various regions in the world have been submitting to the U.N. pertaining to regional nuclear-free zones would be a mockery and a contradiction in terms. For a truly nuclear-free zone presupposes that all the States in the area are nuclear-free and not that some have turned nuclear while others have not. The ratification by States which have not yet signed the ratification instruments would become more indefensible than ever before, within a setting which is blatantly menacing and which would continue to become even more menacing to their vital national interests and existence.

States which are inherently opposed to nuclearization and regard it as anathema *per se* would find themselves compelled, in the face of imminent and ever-growing danger, to seek a protective umbrella from one or the other of the superpowers. This is perfectly understandable, except that it would create a sharp polarization between the superpowers. The price, of course, would be a considerable diminution of *détente* and the onset of situations which may lead to confrontation instead of the presently accepted doctrine of safe competition. The whole non-aligned movement came into existence in the early 1960s to help safeguard the world against super power polarization and the Cold War.

That South Africa and Israel are in the closest atomic collaboration has been established by many sources including the book *The Nuclear Axis* by Zdenek Cervent and Barbara Rogers. Reference is made in the book to the discovery, in August 1977, that South Africa was ready to test its first atomic bomb in the Kalahari desert. *Newsweek* wrote: 'Some U.S. intelligence analysts have concluded that the bomb South Africa had planned to set off had actually been made in Israel.' A high-ranking Washington official was reported as saying: 'I know some intelligence people who are convinced with near certainty that it was an Israeli nuclear device.'

It was a two-way deal, in which Israel obtained from South Africa all its requirements of uranium without any international safeguards or inspection, in exchange for Israeli recycling of the technological know-how, substantially and recklessly imported from the outside. I don't need to elaborate any further, in spite of the secrecy shrouding the collaboration, because available evidence is well-nigh irrefutable.

Was I going to excesses when I argued against the inherent dangers of proliferation which, like a venereal disease, is passed from one party to another and to yet a third in a chain reaction?

The end result, of course, is to place hundreds of millions of people in Africa, Asia and the Middle East in a situation of – to say the least – destabilization and anxiety, leading eventually to a response in kind. Meanwhile, both Israel and South Africa can continue to bask in their intolerable intransigence, illegalities and a false sense of security and superiority. But the 'meanwhile' is a fleeting moment in history and can never last for long.

Total destruction can never bring about real, meaningful or lasting peace. Even the spoils of war in a ravaged continent or subcontinent are hazardous to reap, with radioactive contamination and the scourges of lethal disease.

And yet Israel and South Africa have short-sightedly chosen the path of nuclearization. Indeed, as one authoritative source has argued, the case can be made that the U.S.A., by failing to exercise its undeniable leverage over a country for whose survival it is, in effect, the ultimate guarantor, is actually encouraging proliferation in the Middle East by default.

I am not suggesting that the U.S.A. is happy with what is happening, for it stands to lose most by its continuation. But I *am* suggesting that by permitting the pampered child to become lethal, it is doing a grave error to itself, to its pampered child and to the peace of the world at large.

There are moments in history when major powers must assume major responsibilities, bitter as the medicine may at first seem to be.

The Israelis have always argued that such matters should be the subject of discussion among all the parties concerned. Our position is that the parties concerned are – the whole world. Ratification of the non-proliferation treaty was not contingent upon bilateral discussions between two or more parties. It is an internationally recognized treaty which encompasses all and is open to every State genuinely determined to forgo the nuclear option, under international supervision and inspection.

Secrecy has really worn thin, there is no longer any purpose in pretending that what exists does not exist.[43]

15
The Future

The Palestinians will not simply fade away from the face of the earth. Before this century is out, they will probably be six to seven million uprooted people with a sense of injustice so intense that its bearing on the all-important quest and maintenance of international peace and stability will become unavoidable and, needless to say, disastrous. Let us close this festering wound, and forestall its potentially lethal consequences. I don't know how far ahead in time statesmen formulate their strategies; some are short-sighted, others are identified with muddling through, which may or may not work out. But it is only the far-sighted who can see beyond their noses. Let us hope that the latter will prevail.[17]

In 1980, His Majesty King Hussein paid an official visit to Romania, after which a joint communiqué was issued which dealt with various aspects of the current international situation. President Nicolai Ceausescu and King Hussein in their deliberations on the Middle East reaffirmed that the serious situation prevailing in the Middle East stems from the continuance of Israeli occupation of the Arab territories since 1967 and Israel's refusal to abide by U.N. resolutions. The communiqué, likewise, asserted that the Palestinian question is the core of the conflict in the Middle East. The two leaders were in agreement that the solution must be achieved by immediate and total Israeli withdrawal from all the Arab territories occupied since 1967, including Jerusalem, and the recognition of the national rights of the Palestinian people and their

right to self-determination, their future, including the creation of an
independent State, within the framework of the Security Council
and General Assembly decisions.

The communiqué called for the intensification of the efforts to
bring about a just and lasting solution to the problem of the Middle
East, with the participation of all the parties concerned, including
the P.L.O., and within the framework of the U.N. and on the basis
of its resolutions.

This is the official position of Jordan on the Middle East situation, the crux of which is the redemption of Palestinian national
rights.[49]

I need hardly describe the chaotic financial and economic conditions which presently prevail in Israel because of its military
build-up and belligerent objectives, with inflation and devaluation
running at over 30%.

Its ability, therefore, to commit almost $6 billion for implemen-
tation of the Drobles annexationist plans, already well advanced,
are fuelled by outside assistance.

On 17 June 1980, the U.S. Congressional record has the following excerpt from Senator Stevenson:

> World food and resources are depleting. Nations are stagger-
> ing under the burden of debt. By the hundreds of thousands,
> people are fleeing poverty and oppression. And yet Israel, with a
> high standard of living, is to receive almost as much military and
> economic assistance from the U.S. Government as all the other
> 99.9% of the world's people.

Senator Stevenson, defending his amendment to withhold a mere
$150 million, added:

> This preference for Israel diverts funds from the support of
> human life and vital American interests elsewhere, in an
> interdependent and unstable world . . .
> If it could produce stability in the Middle East, or enhance
> Israel's security, it could be justified but it reflects continued
> U.S. acquiescence in an Israeli policy which threatens more
> Middle East stability, more Israeli insecurity and a continued
> decline of U.S. authority in the world. To say the least, it does

not reflect a balanced consideration of U.S. interests in the world to earmark almost half of all U.S. security assistance for less than one-tenth of 1% of the world's people.

We are asked to authorize this extraordinary sum, notwithstanding the fact that the Begin Government's refusal to settle the Palestinian issue and the status of the West Bank, except on its own terms of annexation for ancient Judea and Samaria, is an obstacle to peace and a cause of continued, if not accelerated, Middle East instability and violence.

The U.S. Government holds the Israeli settlements in occupied territories to be illegal and an obstacle to settlement of the issues that divide Arab and Jew – the fate of the Palestinians. They are inconsistent with Security Council resolution 242 and have been condemned by all members of the Security Council. We consider it to be contrary to international law.

The U.S. position is stated over and over again. The Begin Government blithely, sometimes insultingly, ignores it. It encourages, protects and establishes more Israeli settlements on the West Bank. And the U.S.A. proposes to go on authorizing these remarkable sums for the Begin Government, notwithstanding its defiance of our policy and our interests.

Every time this subject is raised, as it was in the House the week before last, there is a chorus of muted disapproval of Israel's settlement policy, followed by nervous murmurs about being in the midst of a highly delicate peace process which might be upset by doing anything which implies criticism of Israel. The highly delicate process we find ourselves in is a U.S. election campaign. The Congress is always in that delicate situation. That, I fear, is the explanation for the extraordinary sums in this Bill for the Begin Government of Israel.

No matter what the Israeli Government does, even if damaging to the U.S.A. or in violation of agreements with the U.S.A., it gets no embarrassing questions from the U.S.A. The U.S. vote for condemnation of the Israeli settlements policy in the Security Council in March was quickly reversed, once the domestic political implications became apparent to a nervous and divided administration.

Israel attacked the U.S.S. *Liberty* in 1967, killing 34 Americans and causing severe damage to our ship. It may have done so deliberately. Yet the U.S.A. has not recovered compensation for the damage to this ship. I cannot even get a satisfactory report on the incident from the State Department.

Israel's invasion of Southern Lebanon in March 1979 impeded the efforts of the U.N. Interim Force to achieve peace in that country. This was followed by a succession of retaliatory and pre-emptive bombing attacks against Lebanese territory. These military operations were carried out with U.S. equipment, in apparent violation of the terms upon which it was accepted. When Turkey, using U.S.-supplied equipment, invaded Cyprus in 1974, the U.S.A. promptly imposed an arms embargo.

The U.S.A. is subsidizing a settlements policy which undermines the peace process it authored. The actions of the Begin Government in the West Bank conflict with the policy of the U.S.A., the policy embodied in U.N. Security Council resolution 242, the Geneva Convention and the opinion of all other nations on Earth.[59]

In 1947, even though it entailed the dismemberment of a country, it was the U.S.A. which staunchly supported the creation of a Palestine Arab State along with a Jewish State, with Jerusalem and its environs as a *corpus separatum*. This has been the U.S. official policy for 30 years, under eight administrations. And yet, when Israel unlawfully annexed the dwarfed remnants of the real Arab Jerusalem as its capital in 1980, the most that a mighty U.S.A. could do at the Security Council was a timid and apologetic abstention, while all the other 14 members, including its closest allies, voted a resounding censure and condemnation.

May I next present a scenario, projecting the future of the region in the light of the past record and how it will adversely impact upon the potentially phenomenal growth in U.S.–Arab business relationships.

Israel is bent upon a course of conquest, encouraged, undoubtedly, by what cannot be but a temporary military superiority over its immediate neighbours, coupled with unlimited and unconditional military and financial support, direct and indirect, from a U.S.A. which seems to have lost any political or restraining clout over the behaviour of its pampered client.

It is widely suspected that, taking advantage of the U.S.A.'s inability to act in an election year, the flashpoint of a new and disastrous Middle East conflict would be an Israeli military thrust to seize South Lebanon and the waters of the Litani River. This would be done on the pretext of wiping out what Israel terms 'Palestinian terrorists', even though the actual targeted victim would be several hundred thousand Palestinian refugees who are in the Lebanon not by choice but in consequence of their expulsion from their homeland.

If this were to happen, Syria, whose forces are stationed just north, would be unavoidably engaged. Jordan might find itself in danger of encirclement and could not stand idly by. Nor would Iraq or Saudi Arabi which would find themselves in a position of direct geographic confrontation. The Islamic countries of the northern tier, Turkey, Pakistan, Iran and Afghanistan would not and could not tolerate their holiest sites in Mecca, Medina and Jerusalem being in mortal jeopardy, and would react if only because their populations would find themselves denied their all-important religious fulfilment.

This sounds very much like the domino theory, but I am convinced it would most likely unfold over the next few years. Since there is already a substantial American military presence to counter any contingency of Soviet incursion into the oil-rich region, the U.S.A. would find itself imbroiled too. The area could become a new Vietnam, but ten times worse.[57]

We have often been asked: if the current peace process is as intolerable as we state it to be, what positive alternative do we have to offer?

I wish to take this opportunity to stress that the Ninth and Tenth Arab Summit Conferences, while condemning the Camp David Accords, did not reject a peaceful solution to the conflict, but rightly rejected what all 21 Arab States and the representatives of the Palestinian people were unanimous in judging as glaringly unjust and lop-sided, which accommodates the ultimate Israeli objectives of expansion, annexation and dominance, while ignoring a meaningful redemption of the inalienable and sacred rights of the Palestinian people. Although we do not claim we have a panacea for resolving such a conflict, our positive response has been that the peace effort should be put back on the right track and be inspired by guidelines emanating from natural justice; principles prescribed by laws, human and divine; and U.N. resolutions which gave expression and embodiment to those eternal scales of justice.

But a crucial imperative is that it takes two parties to achieve peace. It is of pivotal importance, therefore, that the Israeli leadership and people should engage in deep soul-searching and a fundamental reappraisal of what their real aims and objectives are or should be. For the moment of truth has arrived when basic decisions must be made without ambivalence or equivocation.

As we have been stating repeatedly since 1967, the Israelis can either have the occupied lands or peace, but they cannot have both. Their foremost choice must necessarily be whether or not they opt to live in peace, amity and in conditions of equality and justice with their neighbours. If they are, then all other issues, including security, can be rationally discussed with all the parties directly concerned under U.N. auspices. This may well be a last chance for a peaceful solution for a long time to come.

If Israel chooses the goal of a monolithic and exclusive annexation and hegemony over the whole of Palestine and beyond in a spiral of military expansion, then no time or effort need be expended in wishful thinking. The consequences would inevitably turn a conflict of decades into a struggle of generations.

For our part, we shall reconsider our options, in consonance with our national interest, security and survival. We are confident of the unflinching support of the overwhelming majority of mankind. Our confidence derives from the justice of our cause, the moderation of our course, and the fidelity of the U.N. to its own noble principles, its Charter and the resolutions which are inspired by its letter and spirit. There can and should be no complacency with States which arrogate to themselves the formulation of their own avaricious laws and policies, in total disregard of the mainstream of universal human values.

It is needless for me to reiterate that this applies not only to the question of Palestine and the conflict in the Middle East but, in equal measure, to the plight of our brethren in Namibia, Zimbabwe and other areas where racial oppression is still entrenched. In both instances, injustice, as an Arabic proverb states, might have its day of triumph; but justice will inevitably witness its one thousand days.

In any quest for peace in the Middle East, I feel it imperative to spotlight one critical aspect, which is both regional and universal in dimension, and which weighs heavily on our minds and hearts, as it does on the hearts and minds of thousands of millions of our human race: the fate of Jerusalem, sacred to the adherents of the three monotheistic faiths. Its sanctity even preceded the three great reli-

gions, when it was founded by the Jebusite Semitic Arabs some
5,000 years ago who appropriately gave it the name of Uru-Salem –
the City of Peace.

Being the City of God and Peace, it is inconceivable, repugnant
and blasphemous that it should become the arena of human
conflict, by claims to exclusivity which deny others one of their
most cherished rights.

It should be a haven for benevolence, goodness, devotion and
communion with divine providence. It should be a universal meeting place for all those who believe in the inherent goodness of
mankind. Exclusive sectarian, parochial and terrestrial claims and
ambitions should never compromise its universal message.

I feel compelled to declare that, as far as our people are concerned, we would rather perish than suffer its alienation. Any lasting settlement must never overlook or belittle the intense and
deeply rooted emotions which bind our citizens – both Muslim and
Christian – and our co-religionists of the Islamic World, to this
serene and glorious City of God and Man!

Israeli military withdrawal from Arab Jerusalem is a prerequisite to any just and lasting peace. Freedom of worship, movement
and openness can be guaranteed and assured to the adherents of all
faiths, within a formula of peace as well as collective international
commitment.

There is a world to win and a world to lose by judicious and
prudent approach to the hallowed city of Jerusalem. The world
cannot afford to ignore its fate, its unique message and its ultimate
impact upon world peace and spiritual concord.[45]

My final words are directed at Israel. Israel is presently at the
crossroads and is, therefore, ambivalent and undecided. You have
two options open before you. You have, for the time being, in your
grip, the 'real estate', a not unimportant bargaining point. You are
arming to the teeth with the latest and most lethal weapons. This,
of course, has its price, reflected by a $4 billion deficit in your
balance of payments, continually rising. This militaristic orientation and the siege mentality with which you have saddled yourself
are playing havoc with your internal economy and social equanim-
ity, and may eventually bring about a societal disintegration. You
have even indulged in the perilous pursuit of atomic stockpiling, a
ploy upon which the survival of humanity depends. But as the late
Professor Arnold Toynbee stated, not as a passing opinion, but as

proven historical theory: for every challenge there is a response; the greater the challenge, the greater will be the response. The danger, therefore, is that the belligerency option, no matter how intoxicating temporarily, can never indefinitely remain a one-way traffic. Many on both sides believe in the prophetic inevitability of Armageddon in the heartland of the Holy Land. But to make things less bleak for both of us, and for the world at large, I would like to cite a verse from the Holy Quran which reads: 'A day in your God's calendar is the equivalent of one thousand years in your calculation.' So if any of us has a penchant for self-fulfilling prophecies, let us opt for God's calendar which would, at least, give us and the world an extra thousand years of grace and survival.

The second option is a real peace, provided the inalienable rights of the Palestinians are restored. This does not, as you claim, result in the dismantling of Israel. You have achieved your dream of statehood, and the world has been saying that it will be guaranteed by the Security Council and by the major powers, individually and collectively. You have gathered in all the Jewish refugees, the displaced and numerous others, who belonged to ages-old homelands, but who, for one reason or another, became alienated from them, or so you convinced them by persistent indoctrination.

The rate of immigration to Israel is now a trickle and is further diminished by emigration from Israel. Any further efforts to attract massive new immigration from countries where they are happy, prosperous and powerful would be not only a disaster to themselves, but to Israel itself, from whom it derives such generous and formidable sustenance. Surely you would suffer most, if you dismantled world Jewry.

A change towards peace, primarily with the Palestinians and, by corollary, with the Arab World at large, requires a change of venue on your part, a change of vision, a deep and unprejudiced reappraisal of where your true interests lie.

There are already 1.5 million Palestinians residing in the West Bank, Gaza and Israel. Surely, they are not the monstrous creatures that some of the media you control depict them to be. And enabling the remaining 1.5 million Palestinian refugees to exercise their inalienable right to return or not to return, in phases and in an orderly and organized fashion, over the years, is not the unmitigated disaster you imagine it to be. They are hard-working, skilled and peace-loving on their soil.

If this mutation of premises were given serious consideration by your leadership, and if Palestinians and Israelis lived side by side, in amity and fraternity as the Arabs and Jews did for countless generations, the Middle East and the world might well witness one of its greatest creative transformations.

But let me stress that this can only happen if both you and we unshackle ourselves from the conflicts, tragedies and sufferings of the past few decades. I am thinking in terms of a new order, within a framework of genuine peace, in which the tractor replaces the tank as a way of life and a way of thinking.[6]

The two options are now readily available to you in unmistakable terms. The onus of choice is yours, and the consequences of your decision will be momentous indeed, not only to us and to you, but to the world at large, for decades to come.[10]

Postscript

Once upon a time, a friend of the famous humorist, Hujha, told him that he had some urgent business to do outside the house, and he asked Hujha if he would kindly stand guard at the door to protect the house. Hujha obliged until he got tired of waiting. Not wanting to break his promise to his friend, Hujha pulled out the door which he had consented to protect and, carrying it on his back, went straight to the marketplace. In consternation, the owner of the house saw Hujha in the marketplace and said to Hujha: 'You have promised to guard the house pending my return, and now I see that you have reneged on your promise'; to which Hujha replied: 'No, my friend, I have not; you requested me to guard the door of the house and here it is, safely on my back.' The house, of course, in the meantime was ransacked clean by passing intruders.

And so it is with the question of the Middle East. While the chorus of praise and rationality continues to be echoed in the Security Council and in some foreign offices of the world and while everybody is standing guard over the sanctity and wisdom of resolution 242 and subsequently 338, there is someone within the doorless house who is busy ransacking the house and devouring its inhabitants right down to the bones.[8]

Appendix: Sources and Dates of Speeches